When the Spirit Comes in Power

WHEN THE SPIRIT COMES IN POWER

Rediscovering the Charismatic Dimension of the Christian Life

PETER HERBECK

PUBLISHED BY ST. ANTHONY MESSENGER PRESS
CINCINNATI, OHIO

Scripture verses are taken from the Revised Standard Version of the Bible, copyrighted 1946, 1952, 1971 by the Division of Christian Education of the National Council of Churches of Christ in the USA. Used by permission. Excerpts from the English translation of the *Catechism of the Catholic Church* for use in the United States of America Copyright 1994, United States Catholic Conference, Inc.-Libreria Editrice Vaticana. Used with Permission.

St. Anthony Messenger Press
28 W. Liberty St.
Cincinnati, OH 45202
www.servantbooks.com

Cover design: Steve Eames

04 05 06 10 9 8 7 6 5 4 3 2

Printed in the United States of America
ISBN 1-56955-352-1

Library of Congress Cataloging-in-Publication Data

Herbeck, Peter.
  When the Spirit comes in power : rediscovering the charismatic
dimension of the Christian life / Peter Herbeck.
      p. cm.
Includes bibliographical references.
  ISBN 1-56955-352-1 (alk. paper)
  1. Holy Spirit. 2. Christian life--Catholic authors. I. Title.
  BT121.3.H47 2003
  248.4'82--dc22

2003015067

Dedicated to the loving memory of my father,
Joseph J. Herbeck

With Much Thanks

I owe a great debt of gratitude to all those who have mentored me along the way. There have been many, and all of them have in some way made their contribution to this book. I want to thank all those priests, sisters and lay teachers at Holy Trinity Cathedral in New Ulm, Minnesota, who earned their stripes as they patiently sought to pass on the faith. Thanks also to Dr. John Buri, John Keating, Steve Clark, and others who invested much time in teaching me the ways of a disciple.

Special thanks to Ralph Martin, my longtime friend and colleague who from the first time I heard him preach in the summer of 1978, has played a unique role in helping shape my life as a disciple. As with so many "projects" in my life the past twelve years, his advice and encouragement helped to make this book a reality.

And to the Renewal Ministries family for your zealous commitment to the Lord's call and for putting up with my slightly distracted state during the final stages of the book.

And to my mother Dorothy Herbeck, for her witness of fidelity to Jesus, and for her constant love and prayers, and to my siblings, who have stood by me over these many years, and are always eager to respond to whatever the Lord seems to be doing with us.

Finally, my deepest gratitude goes to my wife Debbie, my best friend who, as always, has walked with me step by step in bringing this book to birth.

Contents

Foreword
BY RALPH MARTIN

There's a remarkable consonance between the fundamental vision unfolded in the documents of the Second Vatican Council, subsequent papal documents, and the reality of the work of the Holy Spirit witnessed to most especially in the Catholic charismatic renewal. Peter Herbeck has done a remarkable job of noting this consonance and exploring its many dimensions.

Peter is one of a handful of today's lay Catholics most equipped to make the connection between the theory and practice of renewal and evangelization. He is well situated to speak with the authority of both study (he holds a M.A. degree in theology with a thesis on the teaching of John Paul II on evangelization) and experience (leader of the mission work of Renewal Ministries). While the documents of Vatican II and the subsequent papal documents on renewal and evangelization are truly extraordinary, there has unfortunately been a vast gap between the theory contained in them and the actual situation of the life of the average Catholic today. Peter's book shows the remarkable things that can happen when theory and practice are brought together in the lives of ordinary people.

The purpose of Peter's book is not to promote a particular movement, but rather the biblical, ecclesial, and pastoral realities witnessed to and embodied in it. Cardinal Suenens, whom Peter cites in this book, one of the four moderators of Vatican II and a leading figure in the integration of charismatic renewal and the wider church, had a remarkable insight into the purpose of charismatic renewal. He often stated that the charismatic renewal wasn't the same type of movement

11

as others in the church (with founders and organizational structures with chains of command), but was rather to be viewed more accurately as a "current of grace," which was witnessing to a reality that belonged to the whole Church and not just a particular movement. It's obvious, but nevertheless important, to say that the Holy Spirit and the gifts of the Spirit aren't the property of a particular movement but belong to the entire Church and to each and every Catholic. Building on this fundamental insight of Cardinal Suenens, Peter maps out in some detail how the experience of God witnessed to in a particular movement, is in fact a providential response to the prayers of Vatican Council II and several popes, to restore to the Church today the essential reality of a "new Pentecost."

It is this "new Pentecost" as Peter so convincingly argues, that is the key to the Church, and individual Catholics, being able to carry out our Christ-given mission in the world today. This is an important book for all concerned for how we as individuals and as a Church can most effectively respond to the great challenges of the aggressive, secular culture that is present everywhere. As Peter makes clear, if we listen to Jesus and avail ourselves of the power of the Spirit, truly wonderful things will unfold.

Introduction

The timing of this book is noteworthy. Its contents have been percolating within me for the past five years, but the opportunity to actually put it into a book didn't surface until Bert Ghezzi, my editor, took me to lunch a year ago and asked me if there was anything stirring in my heart that I wanted to put into writing. I told him that indeed there was. So, when idea met opportunity this book was born.

It was written during the dramatic unfolding of the clergy sex scandal, which is now almost universally recognized as the most significant crisis in the history of the Catholic Church in America. Since the crisis first hit the newspapers there has been a mad scramble to identify its cause and to provide solutions for it.

The debate over the cause of the crisis is wide-ranging. The best diagnosis of the crisis I have read comes from George Weigel's book, *The Courage to Be Catholic.* He said that the crisis is, "most fundamentally, a crisis of discipleship."[1] Though opinions vary greatly as to the cause of the crisis, most everyone agrees that the Church is in need of reform. The question is, "what precisely needs to be reformed?"

Most of the reform debate centers around the need for institutional change. The focus tends to be on the need for policy changes, seminary reform, confronting issues of dissent, and other institutional issues that, no doubt, must be addressed. Yet, institutional reform alone, as important as it is, is not enough.

True reform must go deeper. The word "reform" implies a return to the original "form" of the faith, a returning to the roots or essence of what it means to be a disciple of Jesus Christ. It calls for a rediscovery of those essential elements of faith that have been forgotten or ignored.

13

Calling the current crisis a "crisis of discipleship" touches on the essence of the faith. At the heart of the Christian life is a relationship with a person, Jesus Christ, the only begotten Son of God. A disciple is someone who has entered into a conscious, personal relationship with Jesus Christ. Authentic reform starts with a rediscovery of what discipleship in Christ really means.

I believe that rediscovery has already begun to take place. Pope John Paul II has stated on numerous occasions that the Church, beginning with the Second Vatican Council, has rediscovered the charismatic dimension as one of her constitutive elements. By charismatic dimension he means the present, vital action of the power of the Holy Spirit in the life of each member of the Church.

This rediscovery touches directly upon the "crisis of discipleship" we now face. If we go back to our roots, to the very origin of the Church, we come to Pentecost. Pentecost was an encounter with the power of the Holy Spirit. That experience gave birth to the Church, empowering the apostles to go forward and to bring others into that same contact with the power of the Holy Spirit.

Christian discipleship includes, at its core, a conscious experience of a living, vital relationship with Jesus Christ in the power of the Holy Spirit. The rediscovery of the charismatic dimension of the Church means, in part, the rediscovery of genuine religious experience as a normative aspect of Christian discipleship.

Authentic reform must include the dimension of the personal experience of the power of the Holy Spirit in the life of every believer. If all our attention is focused on institutional reform or on the defense of right doctrine, our attempts at reform will fall short. Right doctrine, sound morality, and institutional reform are necessary elements of an overall reform, but in themselves they are not sufficient.

I believe that if we pay attention to "what the Spirit is saying to the Church" through this rediscovery of the Church's charismatic essence, we will find the key to what the Church most needs now. The

Holy Spirit alone can bring her what she needs: the fire of a renewed Pentecost.

Pope John Paul II has pointed out that the rise of the dynamic movements that have emerged in the Church since the Second Vatican Council are the direct result of the rediscovery of the charismatic dimension of the Church. These movements, though diverse in form, share at least one common characteristic: they produce the kind of fidelity and passion for Christ and his mission that is characteristic of true discipleship. The movements are a word to the Church. They give witness to what happens when we consciously surrender to the present action of the Holy Spirit in our lives. The Holy Spirit wants to release the dynamic power that will make it possible to live the high adventure of Christian discipleship.

The purpose of this book is to underline the irreplaceable fact that the rediscovery of the charismatic dimension of the Church, which constitutes an essential element of the faith, necessarily includes an experience of the risen Christ in the power of the Holy Spirit. The book has an autobiographical aspect as well as testimonies from "Catholics in the pews" whose lives were transformed by the present action of the Holy Spirit.

My hope is that this book can make a small contribution to the debate on the direction of the Church's much needed reform and to inspire all who read it to embrace wholeheartedly the dynamic and profoundly charismatic vision of discipleship presented in the teaching of Pope John Paul II.

ONE

Awakenings

"I have heard your prayers ..."

It was the fall of 1976, my senior year in high school, when my sister Kathy, the oldest of my six brothers and sisters called home with "important news." She said that it was about Dad and that she wanted all of us to be available to talk about his problem with alcoholism. So the next weekend, two of my other siblings who were married, along with my mother, my younger sister, and myself gathered to hear Kathy's news.

I remember being a little bit nervous, feeling awkward, not knowing what to expect from our conversation. It was not typical of my family to sit around the kitchen table together to talk about important family issues, especially issues surrounding my father. Up to that point we were what I would describe as a typical German-Catholic family from small-town America. We attended Catholic school, went to Mass each week, and at least in my case, accepted the faith uncritically. Faith was not something we talked about. We knew what was expected of us and we did it, but we didn't share openly and personally about our faith.

Kathy began by telling us she belonged to a small weekly prayer group in her parish. At their meetings they would take time to pray for one another's needs. For a number of months they had been praying for my father. The previous week, after having prayed for Dad and others, two men came to her, independent of one another, and told her they had a word from the Lord for our family. The word concerned my father and the rest of our family and it went something like this: "I have heard your prayers, where is your faith? Claim the victory I have promised and cling to my word." Kathy said both men were convinced the Lord was going to heal my father but not before our family took this word seriously and believed.

As I listened to her words I was filled with contradictory feelings and emotions. I was uncomfortable just talking about spiritual things in such a personal way. I had never heard anyone talk about receiving "a word from the Lord." How could someone actually hear the Lord? It must have been their imagination at work. Yet at the same time, I knew my sister was not crazy, and the conviction and calm in her voice kept me from dismissing her words as wishful thinking.

Despite the discomfort and awkwardness of the moment, I wanted to believe Kathy. I wanted God to be that real. I wanted him to help our family get free from the one intractable problem that we had lived with all our lives.

My father was an alcoholic. He was the son of an alcoholic. His brother died from an unintentional mixing of prescription drugs with too much alcohol. My great grandfather was an alcoholic. My father returned from World War II, a decorated soldier, having served with distinction in General George S. Patton's Third Army in the Battle of the Bulge. He was a tough tank commander who spoke fluent German and spent most of his four years of service on the front lines. He also returned from the war with a drinking problem. Like many other men, he used alcohol to numb the pain and horror of war that never went away.

My father was a good man and a good father. He loved his family, his community, and his Church. He was a successful businessman, a city councilman, a man who would do anything to help someone in need.

My father's alcoholism cast a dark shadow over our family life. To friends and neighbors we looked like a relatively together family, but on the inside the picture was different. We were broken, sick, and disfigured by the alcoholism. Growing up in an alcoholic home is very strange. There is a great deal of hiding, of make believe, of putting up false fronts in a desperate attempt to smooth over the pain that no one seems to be able to talk about.

When Dad drank, which was usually once or twice a week, he drank hard. When he was sober my father was one of the kindest, most personable men you could ever meet, but when he was drunk he would often be verbally abusive.

There is nothing I wanted more than to see my dad get better. He had been through treatment on a number of occasions, at least one of which was at the insistence of the local court, but nothing really changed. Even our attempt at a family intervention produced no lasting change. He would stop drinking for a month or so but would eventually return to the same pattern. The drinking had continued for so long that I didn't think it would ever change.

Being the last boy at home and less than a year away from college, I was concerned about how my father's drinking would impact my mother and sister once I was gone. Somehow in my adolescent mind, I thought my presence at least made things manageable for everyone. I had prayed many times that something would happen to change the situation before I left home. The summer before my senior year my prayers became more desperate, shifting from a resignation that the whole thing was somehow God's plan for us, the cross we were to bear, to a cry for help that rose from deep feelings of powerlessness and fear.

Kathy's words were a ray of hope for me. Is God hearing our prayers? Can he act here and now? Will he heal Dad? Those were the questions I most wanted answers to, but my sisters kept pressing home the point that Dad was in the Lord's hands and that the larger question now was whether or not we were ready to repent and put the Lord at the center of our own lives. If we did that God would do his part. They believed that our response in faith to the word we had received would make a way for the Lord to do a work in our entire family. Their conviction convinced me that something real was happening.

That night was a turning point for all of us. Later, while lying in bed I cried out to God like never before. I crawled out of bed, got down on my knees and repented for my unbelief. I told the Lord I knew what I had heard from Kathy was his word to me and to our family. I wanted to respond to it with my whole life, but I didn't know how. I wept over the sorry state of my faith, my life, and the broken state of my family. At that moment I experienced a tremendous consolation and assurance that all would be well, that indeed the Lord was near, that he had heard our prayers and he was about to act.

The Breakthrough

About one month later, on a Monday night, I was at home studying. Monday was the night Dad normally drank and this night was no exception. It was late when he came into the dining room where I was working and he sat down next to me. I was waiting for him to give me an earful but he was silent. After a few moments he said, "Peter," staring at me with a glazed look in his eyes. He said, "Peter, I am a sick man and I need help." Then with tears in his eyes, he reached out his hand, "Can you help me, Peter?" I was stunned and shaking. Dad had never admitted he had a problem. It was the first time I could recall ever seeing my father cry. All I could say was, "Yes, Dad. I'll help you, it's going to be OK."

That night Dad went to bed peacefully. He woke up the next morning and called our family physician. The next day he entered treatment at the Johnson Institute at the St. Mary's Extended Care Center in St. Paul, Minnesota.

The Johnson Institute was a family treatment program for chemically dependent people. The Center was world renowned for its groundbreaking work in family-centered drug treatment. Dad entered their six-week inpatient program. One day a week, our family, or "concerned persons" as we were called, joined Dad and those in his group.

The treatment program was eye opening to say the least. Dad's sharing group of about five or six other people were from a wide range of backgrounds, ages, and beliefs. As their counselor put it, "they had only one thing in common, they were drunks." It didn't matter how old or young, rich or poor they were, their lives had become unmanageable because of alcohol. Each of them had heart-wrenching stories to tell about how their abuse of alcohol had destroyed their lives.

Our weekly participation in the program had two dimensions: education and family therapy. The first part of the day was given to educating us on the "disease of alcoholism." We learned about its causes, how it affects a person mentally, physically, emotionally, and spiritually, and its impact on the family unit. I discovered a great deal about Dad and our family during those sessions.

The therapy dimension of the day was much more intense. Each person in my father's group would share something about where they were in their own recovery process. They were working their way through the 12 Steps of the Alcoholics Anonymous treatment program. The first step in the program was for each person in treatment to honestly admit they were powerless over alcohol and that their lives had become unmanageable because of it. Honestly admitting the depth of the problem is the first step to recovery. Most alcoholics live with the deeply held delusion that they have everything under control. They develop an enormous capacity to deny reality in order to continue drinking. The level of dependence for some is so deep their entire world can crumble around them and they still won't admit they have a problem.

These larger group sessions were often very painful. It was hard to hear people's stories and to see their pain. One goal of the treatment process is to get each person to face the mess they have made of their lives. No soft-pedaling, enabling, or candy coating was permitted. The sessions were hard-hitting and at times brutally honest. Within the first few weeks, each of the alcoholics was expected to take a complete moral inventory of their life, writing down everything they possibly could remember about their use and abuse of alcohol. The inventory was supposed to be detailed and completely honest.

During our second week in treatment one of the men in the group was ready to take his next step toward sobriety. He had done his moral inventory and was ready to share it with his family and with all of us. This step serves as a kind of confession and reconciliation for the alcoholic. He pulls out of himself all he can remember, facing courageously for the first time the shame and guilt he carries as a result of his abuse.

The road to this point is so difficult some alcoholics never get there. Those who do often are motivated by a desire to reconcile with their family and to make a new start.

We gathered that day expecting to see a breakthrough for this man and his family. The session was supposed to begin, but the man was the only one from my father's group who wasn't there. The counselor went to check on him to see where he was. A few minutes later the counselor and the man returned. The man looked broken. His eyes were red from crying. He held a letter in his hand. The counselor asked him if he would be willing to read it. He read a letter from his wife and children. All I can remember from that moment was that he said his family wanted nothing to do with him. He was a no-good drunk and from their point of view that's all he would ever be. He was devastated. We all sat in numbed silence watching this man weep bitterly over the loss of his family. He said he no longer had any reason to be sober. My father and the counselor were the only ones in the room who weren't crying that day.

Claiming the Victory

Two weeks later we gathered once again for our group session. It was my father's turn to take the courageous step of publicly acknowledging the truth about his alcohol abuse. I came to the session with high hopes, convinced the key turning point for my father had come. Minutes before the session started my father's counselor asked me what I was so happy about. I told him I thought Dad was going to turn the corner that day. He asked me why I was so confident Dad was ready to face his problem as squarely as he needed to. My response was simple: the Lord told us he was going to heal Dad. My naiveté left him shaking his head in disbelief and commenting, "it's not that easy."

Dad was the first to share. He began to read the details of his drinking inventory. He told us what he drank, where he drank it, and that he had probably lost more than one hundred thousand dollars due to his drinking. Frequent blackouts left him with almost no memory of his behavior while drinking. At a particularly emotional moment he expressed regret for the pain and embarrassment he brought to his family. I remember fighting back tears as he identified our pain. To me it seemed the breakthrough we had hoped for was happening.

Just then Dad's counselor interrupted him and said, "Joe, you're a liar. You've been living a lie for thirty years and you're still lying. You're full of shit and worst of all you're wasting my time and everyone else's with your con game. Why don't you go down to the corner pub, have a few boilermakers, then come back and tell me what you really feel! You don't have the guts to face who you really are."

His words left the entire room shell-shocked. I sat shaking, not knowing whether to cry or to jump up and grab the counselor by the throat. Things seemed to be spinning out of control. My mother and sisters were crying and my father sat with his head down looking pathetically weak. Dad attempted to start over but the counselor wouldn't let him. He told Dad to get out. Literally, he told him he wasn't ready to get sober and that he should leave the Institute because he was wasting everyone's time. Then he looked at the rest of us and said, "we're done."

My mother and I immediately walked up to the counselor wanting to know what he was doing. It wasn't supposed to happen like this. He couldn't be finished. The counselor's words were like a sword cutting through my mother's heart: "I really don't have much hope for Joe." We were crushed. I stood holding my mother in my arms as she wept. We both felt like Dad had reached the end of the road and the victory we had hoped for was lost.

Moments later we gathered back in my father's room. I looked around the room; we were all like lost sheep, confused, dazed, and emotionally drained. My father sat at the edge his bed, with his head bowed in complete silence. He looked defeated and helpless. I will never forget how empty and powerless I felt at that moment. I didn't know what to do next. Suddenly my sister Kathy broke the silence with words that cut through all the confusion. "Listen everybody, this fight is not over. There is spiritual warfare going on right now in this room. The devil is fighting for Dad's soul. He wants to keep our whole family in bondage. We need to fight for Dad, to stand on the Lord's promise to us. We need to repent of our unbelief and to do what the Lord told us. We need to claim the victory he has promised."

That was the first time I had heard anyone speak so directly about spiritual warfare. I didn't quite know what it all meant, but I knew without a doubt we were in a fight. We were up against a real power, something that had a hold of us and didn't want to let go. Looking back, knowing what I know now, I can see how the Lord was leading us to this moment of confrontation. He was teaching us, revealing to us the same truths he taught his disciples: we're in a war against a real enemy who is more powerful than we are, and because of our sin, we've allowed him to enslave us. It's a battle we cannot win on our own resources.

Though I couldn't see it at the time, the entire scene in my father's room was a moment of truth. The reason I felt so weak and powerless was because I am weak and powerless. The irony is that precisely at the moment I thought we had lost all hope, hope was born. The circumstances of my father's condition stripped us of the illusion of strength and forced us to confront our powerlessness, and there, as Jesus promises, we found our strength.

When Kathy finished what she had to say, another one of my sisters suggested we hold hands and pray. We reached out to each other and prayed the most honest and desperate, yet faith-filled prayer we had ever prayed together. We confessed our unbelief, we acknowledged our powerlessness, and we thanked God for the victory he had won for our family. The prayer was simple and heartfelt, with no accompanying signs of some spiritual breakthrough. We did it because we had no other place to turn.

A few minutes later we said our good-byes to Dad and spoke briefly with his counselor who was still contemplating the possibility of releasing Dad early from the program. He had serious doubts as to whether my dad was ready to change.

I drove home that night and through the rearview mirror I could see my mother crying in the back seat. When I asked her why she was crying she said, "I feel so bad for your father. He's trying so hard, but I just don't think he can do it." I wanted to say something that would help relieve her pain, but even words of spiritual encouragement seemed hollow. I had my own doubts about how it would all end.

The next day we received a call from Dad's counselor. He said that something new was going on in Dad. He and Dad had stayed up late into the night and for the first time my father began to be totally honest about his addiction. We returned to the hospital and as soon as I saw Dad I knew something had happened. He looked different. His countenance had changed and there was hope in his eyes. He hugged me and said that everything was going to be OK.

Two weeks later my father stood up in front of a room full of patients and their families and said, "I'm Joe Herbeck and I'm an alcoholic." He acknowledged that his life had become unmanageable and that from then on he could remain sober only with the help of God and his family. We went home that day together with renewed hope and a deeper conviction about the reality of the Lord's living presence in our lives. I didn't realize it at the time, but that day was only the beginning of a much deeper process of spiritual awakening for our entire family.

"Cling to My Word ..."

Within the next few years the character of our family gatherings changed. We had always spent the holidays together. I have good memories of those days, but like most families they were filled primarily with good food, games, and watching sports on television. After our experience in treatment we talked more and even started praying spontaneously together, asking the Lord to continue to help us on our journey.

What was most remarkable about the change was how comfortable we felt about sharing our faith. It was awkward at times for some, but we began to speak openly about Jesus and his plan for our lives. On some occasions we spent hours sharing, praying for each other, and ministering the love of the Lord to one another. Family time evolved into some of the richest, most intense spiritual times of the year. Jesus had gradually become the center of our family life.

During those years all seven of us Herbeck children grew tremendously in our faith. Even those family members who hadn't been to church in years came back to the Lord. Our family had grown to include thirty grandchildren and we had a growing conviction that the Lord wanted to break the cycle of addiction that had plagued my family for generations.

As I write this story today, twenty-three years later, I can say that the Lord has broken that cycle of addiction. None of my father's children have become addicted to drugs or alcohol, and of the thirty-five grandchildren and great grandchildren only one has had a drinking problem. A friend of mine who has directed a drug treatment program for more than fifteen years told me what happened to my family was a miracle. He said that in all his years of running a treatment program he had never heard of such a complete break occurring in a family where alcohol addiction had been so deeply ingrained for generations.

My father died of cancer in November of 1997. He lived sober, one day at a time for all those twenty years. Those were the most fruitful years of his life. He served the community he loved as a city councilman for sixteen of those twenty years. During that time he saw the spiritual transformation of his family. It was my father's weakness and the broken condition of our family that became the doorway to a new life together in Jesus.

Just two days before my father died my brothers and sisters and I had an opportunity to be with Dad together one last time. Cancer was ravaging his body, beginning in his lungs then spreading to his brain and then to his bones. The morphine patch the nurse had given him helped abate what would have been unbearable pain. Seeing him in that broken condition, with death slowly, steadily having its way with him was overwhelming for me. It was the first time I was that close to death.

As each of my brothers and sisters said their good-byes to Dad I leaned my head gently on his shoulder and wept. I was crushed with sadness as I could feel death consuming him. It all felt so dark. Death seemed so big and so overwhelming, it reduced all of us to complete powerlessness. Dad was fading away and we could do nothing about it. At that moment my sister Barb asked Dad if he would like to lead us in prayer one more time. He barely had the strength to speak, but he managed to lead us first with the Our Father, then a Hail Mary. The last prayer we ever prayed together was his favorite, the Serenity Prayer: "God grant me the serenity to accept the things I cannot change, to have the courage to change the things I can, and to have the wisdom to know the difference."

While we prayed that final prayer I sensed a light penetrating the darkness of the moment. As we knelt around Dad we were all overcome with sadness, yet we knew that the Lord was present. In this moment of complete powerlessness, the light of the Lord began to shine in the darkness for us. I knew like I had never known before that nothing can separate us from the love of God in Christ Jesus. The words the Lord had given us twenty years earlier filled my heart: "Where is your faith? Claim the victory I have promised and cling to my word."

The victory Jesus promised is victory over death. I understood that the whole experience of transformation we had undergone the previous twenty years had prepared us for this moment. I felt his power lift me, giving me strength to claim the victory he was winning for Dad, even as Dad's strength was wasting away. Jesus was perfecting his power in Dad's weakness.

As he slipped in and out of consciousness over the next forty-eight hours, we could hear Dad crying out to Jesus time and again. He died peacefully in the middle of the night with my sister Kathy at his side.

TWO

A Whole New World

My father's journey toward sobriety was the doorway through which the Lord Jesus led me into a deep, personal encounter with him. Many times over the years I've thought about how our family's greatest weakness, the source of generational bondage and brokenness we grew up in, became the very thing the Lord used to bring us into a deeper relationship with him.

My mother asked me to give the eulogy at my father's funeral. As I pondered the many achievements I could highlight from Dad's life—the military honors he received for heroic service during World War II, his business successes and civic leadership, what became abundantly clear to me was that the most fruitful, lasting achievement came not from his successes but from his failures. The most valuable and enduring legacy my father left us was born out of brokenness.

When Dad finally admitted that he was powerless everything began to change. The decision to surrender, that moment when he openly acknowledged that his life had become unmanageable and that he had made a terrible mess of things, is the point at which the Lord began to take center stage. We all gradually began to acknowledge the reality of our own desperate state. We were facing something that was too big for us, family demons that had held sway for generations.

It was right there, in the midst of the brokenness, that I began to experience an awakening of my own faith. I remember how frightening it was when we all began to speak more openly about the effects alcohol addiction had on our lives. Like most families living with addiction we spent years living in denial and hiding from the truth about ourselves. Admitting that we were diseased, that is, deeply affected by a distorted, sick view of reality was hard to face. It was scary, lonely, confusing, and humiliating, especially at seventeen.

There was a direct correlation between my own experience of brokenness and the intensification of prayer and seeking God. Up to that point in my life I prayed on occasion and mainly for things I wanted—success in sporting events, help on exams, and for things, like a motorcycle or a pair of tennis shoes. The prayer was shallow, because that's where I lived at the time. Facing the truth about our addiction plunged me into the deep. I began to cry out to God with real desperation. I felt his light beginning to shine on me and I didn't like what I was seeing. The change we were undergoing as a family wasn't just about Dad and his problem. All of us had walked in the shadows and were now being called into the light of the Lord.

In those moments of desperation I began to seek answers to the larger questions of life: Who am I? Why am I here? Where have I come from? Is there some larger purpose in my life? Where is my life headed? At eighteen I couldn't answer most of those questions. In fact, up to that point in my life such questions hadn't crossed my mind. Most of my early teen years were spent testing the limits. I knew that now things had to change. Through the treatment process I was required, like my father, to take a "searching moral inventory" of my life. That inventory brought me to the sobering realization that my life had no real direction.

During this time my sisters would periodically encourage me to pray, to read the Bible, and to ask the Holy Spirit to take control of my life. One day my sister Dena called to invite me to join her for what she called a "charismatic Mass" at the local parish the following Tuesday night. Mass on a weeknight seemed strange enough, but what was a charismatic Mass? She said she really couldn't explain it but she assured me that I would enjoy it and that it would help me. I agreed to join her.

My experience of the Mass was uneventful but memorable

nonetheless. The first thing I noticed was that I was the only guy my age there and that most of the hundred or so people there were middle-aged or elderly women. The second thing I noticed was how free they were to express themselves in worship. They raised their hands, smiled a lot and said, "Praise the Lord" quite a few times. The whole thing felt a bit awkward, but I tried to make the most of it.

At the end of the Mass, the man who was leading the music ministry stood up and said there was one seat left on the bus to the National Charismatic Conference to be held later that summer at the University of Notre Dame. My sister immediately turned to me and said, "that seat is for you!" She had never been to it, but had heard that thousands of people attended and that there were inspiring speakers, and healings and miracles. The whole thing seemed a bit much for me but the idea of attending a conference at the football stadium at Notre Dame had real possibilities. Two months later I was on the bus heading to South Bend for the conference along with two or three other men and about forty women. The conference was unlike any other religious or church-related event I'd ever been a part of. There were almost thirty-five thousand people gathered in the football stadium on a hot August night. I will never forget the intensity of the enthusiasm and the joyful worship. Everyone, men and women alike, were singing with all their hearts and raising their hands in praise of God. I had never seen so many priests in one place; there must have been two hundred fifty gathered on the floor of the stadium, joining fully in the jubilant, festive praise.

One thing I knew for sure, these folks had something I did not have. The joy, freedom of expression, and the conscious personal relationship with Jesus was different. The entire focus of the worship, preaching, testimonies, and general conversation was the person of Jesus. People spoke of him as if they knew him. To them he was a living Jesus, someone who acted in their lives, and knowing him actually made a difference in their lives.

Through our family's experience with my father and the help of my sisters I had gotten a taste of the reality of Jesus' presence and power. I knew he was calling me and that I had already begun to undergo change in my life, but I wanted more. I didn't know exactly what that meant or how to get it, I just knew I wanted it. Later that night I told my roommate, a veteran of a number such conferences, how different it all seemed and that I really longed to know Jesus in the way others seemed to know him. He laughed and told me not to worry because, "nobody comes to one of these things with an open heart and leaves without encountering Jesus in the power of his Holy Spirit." He told me to relax and let the Lord lead me through the weekend.

The next day was an altogether different experience. It was a teaching day. The workshops and general sessions I attended were like undergoing a surgical procedure on my heart and mind. The preaching I heard that day cut me wide open. The speakers' words were like lasers cutting through me, exposing the condition of my heart. I had never heard the word of God preached with such force, clarity, power, and relevance. I could literally feel the power of the Spirit touching me, confirming the words being spoken, creating in me a hunger for more.

During the afternoon workshop, the words of Fr. Francis Martin and a well-known Protestant preacher named Ern Baxter astounded me. They preached about the humility of Jesus, his Passion, death, and resurrection, as well as the beauty, power, and majesty of his resurrected life. Before they even finished I was undone. A spirit of conviction came upon me, and a cry of repentance began to stir in me. I saw the condition of my heart in the light of Jesus' death on the cross. I saw the effects of my own sin. My heart seemed small and atrophied, hardened by rebellion and indifference toward God. For so long I had ignored God, chasing after sins of the flesh, self-indulgence, rebellion, and the approval of friends.

I felt such conviction that I left the session early to find a priest who could hear my confession. I had gone to confession over the years on occasion, but I had never really confronted the truth of my own rebellion against God and my refusal to follow his commands. That day was different. My presumption before God collapsed into a sea of tears for my failure to give him what he deserved, namely, my love, loyalty, and trust. So much of what I had done with my life came rushing to my mind that afternoon and I dumped it all at the feet of Jesus, who was there for me in the person of a kind, gracious priest.

For the first time in my life I felt washed, cleansed by the grace of the sacrament. Jesus' love overwhelmed me that day. A new faith was birthed in my heart through the preaching of the gospel. St. Paul says the "the word of God is living and active, sharper than any two-edged sword, piercing to the division of soul and spirit, joints and marrow, and discerning the thoughts and intentions of the heart. And before him no creature is hidden, but all are open and laid bare to the eyes of him with whom we have to do" (Hb 4:12-13). I experienced that truth in a vital, life-changing way that day. The word of God exposed the true condition of my heart. Jesus came to me in the bold, unabashed preaching of those men, and he revealed to me the truth about myself that was hidden from my own eyes but lay bare before his gaze.

There was something different about my confession on that day. I had felt guilt before and confessed particular sins in confession, but I had never before known such deep sorrow and sadness for the overall condition of my heart before God. How could I give such a paltry, pathetic, stingy, indifferent response to so great a love? Why did I love sin so much? Why did I put so much weight on things that didn't matter at all? How could I be so blind as to ignore the one thing that mattered the most? The amazing thing about that experience was the complete lack of condemnation I felt. I felt the love of Christ washing over me. Something new was happening in me and I knew I wasn't creating it through my own willpower or emotion. God was doing something. Later a verse from St. Peter's first letter described what I had experienced: "you have been born anew, not of perishable seed but of imperishable, through the living and abiding word of God.... that word is the Good News which was preached to you" (1 Pt 1:23, 25).

That day I had an experience of waking up to a new spiritual reality. As I lay in bed I wondered if this connection to the Lord that day would last. Knowing my own weakness and having experienced making promises to God in the past—promises I hadn't kept, I was genuinely concerned about whether I would be able to live in accord with what I was hearing that weekend.

The concluding Mass of the conference was held on Sunday in the stadium. The theme of the conference was, "You Shall Be My Witnesses." A priest who described his experience of evangelizing Buddhist monks in Japan a few years earlier gave the homily. He talked about the dramatic conversions and signs and wonders that the monks had experienced. What stood out to me was the dynamic way this priest lived his faith. He communicated a deep trust in God and an expectation that the Lord would use him to help extend his kingdom, even in difficult situations like the one he encountered in Japan.

As Communion approached, I prayed intensely, asking the Lord for the gift of faith. I confessed my weakness and pleaded with the Lord to give me the grace to live by faith. On my own strength I was like the man described in Scripture that looked at himself in the mirror and walked away only to forget what he looked like. I had begun to see the Lord in a new way that weekend, and I didn't want to walk away and forget what I had experienced.

As I went up to Communion I asked for that single gift, for a genuine, enduring faith. As I returned to my seat I stood with my eyes closed repeating that same prayer. At that moment I felt someone tap me on the shoulder. A man I had never met was standing next to me. He said that he was sitting about six rows behind me and that while I was standing in line for Communion he saw me and he felt a very strong urge from the Holy Spirit to come and tell me something. He told me, "The Lord Jesus wants you to know that the faith and love that you seek shall be granted to you because he loves you and has died for you!"

As soon as he spoke those words I felt a tremendous rush of power from my head to my toes. I felt an intense heat running through my body accompanied by a vivid experience of the presence of the risen Christ. It seemed to me that the Lord was present, that he was drawing near and that the closer he came the more overwhelming and total the experience became. My heart was filled to overflowing with joy and an experience of Jesus' personal love for me. In that moment, without thinking I reached out to the man who had spoken to me and I embraced him. I began to weep tears of joy. I couldn't believe how real Jesus seemed, how present, how personal and powerful was his presence. As I hung on to the man I remember looking up, my eyes filled with tears, and seeing a stadium filled with the power of the presence of Jesus. Everywhere I looked it seemed people were being touched by the presence of Jesus in the power of the Holy Spirit. Just then I heard the voice of the Lord, not an audible voice, but an interior voice, clear and direct, in a way I had never heard it before, yet I knew it was Jesus. He said, "Welcome, the reign of God is at hand, you are part of a whole new order, my Kingdom."

I immediately began to praise Jesus in a new way. I sang his praises, and acclaimed him with shouts of gladness at the top of my lungs. I raised my hands and began to dance with joy. It was spontaneous, natural, free, and unselfconscious. It was as though the reality of what I was experiencing internally needed, indeed, demanded an external expression. The encounter of Jesus' presence in the power of the Holy Spirit released an interior dynamism and energy that simply burst forth in spontaneous praise.

A flood of words came pouring through me: "Worthy, worthy, worthy are you Lord! You are holy, awesome, powerful, amazing, beautiful, and wonderful!" The words were on my tongue before I could put them together in my mind. It was as if a wellspring were tapped in my heart and it exploded forth and just kept flowing. The amazing thing was that it all felt so natural and effortless. It wasn't just emotion or enthusiasm, but it was more than that. It was something profound, which was touching the core of my being.

That day changed my life permanently. The Lord gave me a new gift, a life-changing experience of his power and presence. He released in me a faith I had never known before. I met him in a deeply personal way and that new knowledge changed everything.

On the long bus ride home to Minnesota I couldn't stop talking about what happened. As I shared my experience it seemed everyone had a similar experience. The Lord had truly touched everyone in a way that seemed to answer their deepest longings. How could Jesus be so personally present, saying and doing different things, in such a life-changing way to a multitude of people at the same time? I was astounded by the reality of Jesus' power.

The next morning my mother met me at our back door. She asked me how the conference went but I didn't know how to explain to her what had happened, especially since she had never been to a "charismatic" service. My mother had always had real faith. She prayed her rosary daily and read the Scriptures. She was a faithful friend of Jesus and Mary. I tried to describe to her what happened, but all I could do was cry. She embraced me and said, "it's all right, Peter, you don't have to tell me, I already know, I prayed for this all your life."

Genuine Change

The days following the conference were less intense from an experiential point of view, but there was no doubt that something strong and enduring had taken place. The enduring quality of the experience is what set it apart from anything else I had ever known. Something fundamental had changed in me. My thought life, interests, desires, and dreams were different. I had a new hunger for God, for Scripture, for the sacraments, and most of all, an intense passion to want to share with others what the Lord had done for me.

The most noticeable change was the experience of an interior strength or new power to say no to old habits of living in the world. Up to that point, even the period immediately following my father's time in treatment, I lived in the "twilight." That is, I had a measure of faith and a genuine desire to know God, but I had a lingering affection for the world and old habit patterns of sin that I didn't want to relinquish. My life as a Catholic was very inconsistent. I was constantly taking one step forward and two steps back. At times I had wanted to change and had even made resolutions to do so, but it wasn't long before I would find myself falling right back into old sinful habits.

I was what the Scriptures describe as a "double-minded man, unstable in all his ways." My heart was divided. Because of my affection for sin I lived with one foot in each kingdom, straddling between the call of God and the desires of my flesh. Too often, the power of the flesh won out. C.S. Lewis, in his powerful essay, "The Weight of Glory," gives a precise description of this double-mindedness: "We are half-hearted creatures, fooling about with drink, sex and ambition when infinite joy is offered us ... we are far too easily pleased ... you and I have need of the strongest spell that can be found to wake us from this evil enchantment of worldliness that has been laid upon us."[1] I needed "the strongest spell" to awaken me from the "enchantment of worldliness" that kept me living in the twilight.

The experience of the Spirit was like coming into the light. It was a new dawn, a new day. Standing in the stadium amidst all that passionate faith and single-hearted devotion, while hearing the truth proclaimed clearly, left me exposed. It was the light of faith and truth that allowed me to see the condition of my own heart and mind. It was the convincing power of the Holy Spirit that awakened me from slumber.

And it was the conscious awareness of the abiding presence of the

Spirit that gave me the desire and new power to live in the daylight. I knew things would be different because I knew the presence of the Holy Spirit in a new way. I felt a new confidence because I knew that the Holy Spirit was with me and that he was a real person who wanted to be with me, to guide me in the way I should go.

I was able to say no to old habits because the Holy Spirit began to change my desires. Everything didn't change overnight, nor did all temptation flee. But real change did begin to take place almost immediately. The fear of talking to friends about my faith completely disappeared. I began to talk to everyone about the love of Jesus and the power of the Holy Spirit. A few of my buddies thought I was crazy, but I didn't care. Up to that point I never had a consistent prayer life. I almost never read the Scriptures and only occasionally set time aside to sit down and pray. Now, I began to pray everyday. A deep hunger for Scripture grew in me and I began to read and study it almost every day, sometimes for hours. I started going to daily Mass and regular confession.

As my hunger for the Lord began to grow, my desire for things of the world began to die. Things that I once considered cool, late night partying, rock concerts, making the social scene, just didn't interest me anymore. I remember one friend saying to me, "Herbeck, what's happened to you. You don't want to party anymore? Man, have you changed!" I told him what happened to me and that there were certain things we used to do that I didn't ever want to do again. He just stared at me with a look of disbelief and said, "You got religion?" This friend and others decided they liked the old Herbeck better, so we ended up gradually going our separate ways. That was difficult, but what really surprised me was to find that other friends responded positively and as a result our friendships reached a depth we previously didn't know was possible.

I began attending a charismatic prayer meeting at the local parish. Like that charismatic Mass, the prayer group was composed of mostly middle-aged women, but I was so hungry to learn more that being the only nineteen-year-old guy didn't bother me. The ladies were very kind to me; they gave me books and tapes that helped me understand the grace that was unfolding in my life. I'm very thankful for all that the members of that little prayer group did for me. It was through them that I eventually met other young men who became companions for me on the road the Lord had laid out for me.

A New Pentecost

In 1998, Pope John Paul II gathered in Rome with some five hundred thousand members of the more than fifty lay movements that have emerged in the Catholic Church since the Second Vatican Council. It was Pentecost, in the year of the Holy Spirit, designated as such by the Holy Father as a means of preparing the entire Church to enter the Great Jubilee Year 2000, the beginning of the Third Millennium.

That day the Holy Father read the signs of the times and gave his perspective on what he saw the Holy Spirit doing in our time. As he had done on other occasions, he pointed to the Second Vatican Council as a great gift of the Holy Spirit for our time, a kind of spiritual watershed and turning point for the Church. He began by saying, "Whenever the Spirit intervenes, he leaves people astonished. He brings about events of amazing newness; he radically changes persons and history. This was the unforgettable experience of the Second Vatican Ecumenical Council during which, under the guidance of the Spirit, the Church rediscovered the charismatic dimension as one of her constitutive elements...."[2]

This is an extraordinary reading of the signs of the times, a perspective we will look at in more detail in upcoming chapters, but for now, I simply want to point out its personal significance. When I read the Holy Father's words I understood exactly what he was talking about. Immediately I felt a direct correlation between his reading of what the Spirit is doing in our time and my life-changing experience at the University of Notre Dame twenty years earlier. He gave a perfect description of what happened to me. When the Spirit touched me that day, he left me "astonished." He brought about in me "events of amazing newness"; indeed, he "radically" changed my life.

The Holy Father has called this "rediscovery of the charismatic dimension" of the Church "the grace of a renewed Pentecost."[3] This has happened to literally tens of millions of people across the world since the Council. We are living at a moment of "Pentecostal renewal," a time in which the Lord himself is pouring out his Holy Spirit in order to produce in his people precisely what he produced in his apostles on the first Pentecost. "Pentecost," according to Pope John Paul II, "was not only a moment of intense emotion; it was the start of a dynamism of supernatural origin which developed throughout the Church's history."[4]

Pentecost is the release of dynamic power. The "rediscovery of the charismatic dimension" of the Church is precisely a renewed experience of this "dynamism of supernatural origin." And, it includes but is not exhausted by "a moment of intense emotion." Again, he is describing what I experienced. The encounter with the Holy Spirit included the experience of intense emotion, but it did not end there. The emotion was simply the immediate result of knowing I was being touched by "a dynamism of supernatural origin." The heart of the Pentecostal experience is not emotion, but a changed life, a renewed life in the Holy Spirit.

This story, retold millions of times in the past thirty years, is the story of the personal experience of the grace of the Baptism in the Holy Spirit. This grace gave rise to the worldwide movement known as the charismatic renewal. Today, in the United States, the movement itself has begun to fade, especially when compared to the explosive growth that characterized it from the late '60s to the late '70s. But the reality of the baptism in the Holy Spirit has not. The "rediscovery of the charismatic dimension" of the Church continues throughout the world.

The remainder of this book is dedicated to providing a deeper understanding of this Pentecostal grace. We are living in the midst of a "rediscovery" of what the Holy Father describes as an "essential" element of the Church's life. The charismatic dimension of our life as believers is not something that belongs on the periphery of our faith, but touches its core. It's the very essence of the Church, not something accidental, but rather something that defines what she is, and what we are as members of the Church. Because of that fact, all of us are being summoned to take up this journey of rediscovery in order that we might hear more clearly what the Spirit is saying to the Church in our time.

THREE

The Challenge of Religious Experience

In the early '90s I helped sponsor an evangelistic rally in a large sports hall in Eastern Europe. Thousands of people of all ages packed the hall for the one-day event.

The vast majority of those in attendance had never been to a religious event of this kind. In fact, due to the oppressive demands of the former Soviet regime, such an event would have been illegal. Because of decades of religious oppression there was a lingering sense of paranoia and discomfort in some. Participating in a religious event in a public place, outside a church building, was unusual. We used the sports hall in order to reach people who hadn't seen the inside of a church in years, maybe in their lifetime.

The goal of the day was simple: to proclaim the gospel of Jesus Christ in the power of the Holy Spirit. The day began in a somewhat stiff, subdued tone. From the stage, the majority of people looked uncomfortable, but as the gospel was preached and testimonies were shared, the atmosphere gradually began to change. I could see that the initial self-consciousness gave way to a genuine openness and receptivity to the message. As the gospel was preached I could sense the Holy Spirit touching people throughout the crowd. Their faces began to change and the sadness and fear that was deeply etched in the countenances of so many turned to joy. Some wept quietly as they heard the message of Jesus' personal love for them. Others bowed their heads in prayer, some fell to their knees in response to the message they were hearing.

At one point, the presence of the Holy Spirit was so strong we decided to stop speaking from the stage for a brief moment and let the Holy Spirit do with us whatever he wanted. I invited everyone who so desired to close their eyes in silence and gently pray a prayer welcoming the Holy Spirit more fully into their hearts. The entire arena grew silent. After a few moments, people wept spontaneously, and many stood up with their hands raised in the air. Within a few moments just about everyone, other than those who were still kneeling, stood up and began to raise their hands or to clap or shout with joy. Some began to shout, "Jesus, Jesus, Jesus!"

I asked the music ministry to lead us in a series of songs expressing gratitude to God. The entire arena exploded with one voice in songs of praise. The atmosphere was electric. People danced, waved their hands, and some even jumped up and down. Their faces were radiant. The words of the psalmist went through my mind as I looked out over the crowd, "Thou hast turned for me my mourning into dancing; thou hast loosed my sackcloth and girded me with gladness, that my soul may praise thee and not be silent" (Ps 30:11-12).

In the midst of this joyful expression of praise, one of our team members whispered into my ear a conviction he had that the Lord wanted us to pray with people suffering from alcohol and drug addiction, severe migraine headaches, as well as eye and ear problems. Over the next hour or so we prayed for people suffering from those and other ailments. Some people experienced immediate relief. A woman who was almost completely blind in one eye was able to see again. At least five people experienced the recovery of all or some of their hearing. A number of people suffering from long term, debilitating migraines experienced immediate relief.

The greatest healing that happened that day was that hundreds of people who had rejected their faith or who had never practiced it began the journey home to the Lord and to his Church. The local organizers were ecstatic. In their words, "they never dreamt that such a thing was possible—especially in a former Soviet country."

The day ended with the celebration of Mass led by the local bishop and a dozen priests from the diocese. At the end of Mass the bishop, priests, and servers processed out during the closing song, as is our custom in the Catholic Church. When the song ended, no one wanted to leave, so the music ministry kept playing. After a few minutes the priests came back up on the stage. The joyful praise and dancing continued for almost an hour before we finally drew the day to a close.

During that final time of prayer I noticed something that seemed very unusual. The priests who were standing on the stage weren't singing. In a dramatic contrast to the rest of the arena, the priests were standing, some with their arms folded, with a stoic look on their faces. All around them people were smiling, dancing, and singing at the top of their lungs, but they stood there apparently unaffected. I assumed that they were somehow unhappy with the whole experience.

Later, in speaking to a few of their fellow priests they assured me they approved of the day, in fact some of them had been deeply touched by the event, but it also presented a challenge. They didn't know how to respond. They had been taught in the seminary to mistrust "enthusiastic" expressions of religious experience. Such activity was a form of emotionalism, and as such, was spiritually imbalanced and usually doctrinally unsound. They didn't want to look like the very "enthusiasts" they had been cautioned about in their formation.

An *a Priori* Bias ...

To exercise caution regarding religious experience is prudent. All the spiritual writers in the Catholic mystical tradition warn against an excessive focus on religious experience and the need to apply solid discernment when we encounter spiritual phenomena. They warn us that spiritual phenomena and religious experience, even when authentic, can, if not handled properly, lead to a range of problems. An imbalanced approach to religious experience can lead to an excessive focus on oneself, rather than love of God and neighbor, which every authentic religious experience is properly ordered to.

Yet, despite their consistent warning, the mystical writers understand that religious experience is a normal part of the Christian life. In fact, their warnings assume it. Indeed, their own lives were replete with a wide range of religious experience and genuine encounter with the living God. The focus of their writing was often that living encounter, which necessarily entails some dimension of religious experience, whether it be dreams, visions, experience of spiritual ecstasy, the spiritual marriage, prophecy, miracles, etc. They not only provide principles to guide the spiritual journey, their works are often a record of the wide range of spiritual experience a disciple will likely encounter along the way.

To put it simply, the Catholic "experts" on spiritual experience, the mystical writers of the Church, do not see religious experience as a negative, as something to be avoided at all costs. They don't reduce it all to mere emotion or superficiality or a distraction found primarily among the spiritually weak and immature. Nor are they uncomfortable with religious experience.

The disposition of these great writers toward religious experience is, in my opinion, much different than the prevailing attitude among many in the Church today. There seems to be an *a priori* bias against religious experience. Much like my priest friends from Eastern Europe, Catholics tend to be uncomfortable with religious experience, especially when it includes an emotional component. Religious experience is something that happens to saints and mystics; it's for the chosen few, the monks and contemplatives, the really "holy" people. As one contemporary writer put it, "generations of ordinary lay Catholics have imbibed the notion that the spiritual life is essentially one of moral striving and formulaic prayer, apart from any direct experiential contact with God and his saving deeds."[1]

Why this attitude toward religious experience predominates today and how exactly we arrived here are very interesting questions, but they are questions I will leave to others who are better equipped to answer them. My point here is to draw out the dramatic contrast between the attitude typical among Catholics today and the clear picture of the normative quality of religious experience found in the Scriptures, the writings of the Church Fathers and the saints throughout the history of the Church.

The Scriptures are full of accounts of religious experience. The whole New Testament, especially the Acts of the Apostles and the letters of St. Paul, are a record of the early Church's encounter with the living God through the experience of the Holy Spirit. Contemporary biblical scholar Luke Timothy Johnson said, "the New Testament is remarkable among ancient religious texts for its high proportion of first-order discourse about experience." He notes that, "it takes considerable effort to read through the pages of the New Testament without encountering statements and claims about what the writers and readers were either experiencing or had already experienced ... it is literally impossible to read the New Testament at any length without encountering claims that something is happening to these people, and it is happening *now*."[2]

Consider just of few examples from the Acts of the Apostles:

"When the day of Pentecost had come.... suddenly a sound came from heaven like the rush of a mighty wind, and it filled all the house where they were sitting" (Acts 2:1-2).

"And when they had prayed, the place in which they were gathered together was shaken; and they were filled with the Holy Spirit and spoke the word of God with boldness" (Acts 4:31).

"But he, full of the Holy Spirit, gazed into heaven and saw the glory of God, and Jesus standing at the right hand of God; and he said, 'Behold, I see the heavens opened, and the Son of man standing at the right hand of God" (Acts 7:55-56).

"Now as he journeyed he approached Damascus, and suddenly a light from heaven flashed about him. And he fell to the ground and heard a voice saying to him, 'Saul, Saul, why do you persecute me?' And he said, 'Who are you Lord?' And he said, 'I am Jesus, whom you are persecuting'" (Acts 9:3-5).

"And he (Peter) became hungry and desired something to eat; but while they were preparing it, he fell into a trance and saw the heaven opened, and something descending, like a great sheet, let down by four corners down upon the earth" (Acts 10:10-11).

"While Peter was still saying this, the Holy Spirit fell on all who heard the word. And the believers from among the circumcised who came with Peter were amazed, because the gift of the Holy Spirit had been poured out even on the Gentiles. For they heard them speaking in tongues and extolling God. Then Peter declared, 'Can any one forbid water for baptizing these people who have received the Holy Spirit just as we have?'" (Acts 10:44-47).

"And a vision appeared to Paul in the night: a man of Macedonia was standing beseeching him and saying, 'Come over to Macedonia and help us.' And when he had seen the vision, immediately we sought to go on into Macedonia, concluding that God had called us to preach the gospel to them" (Acts 16:9-10).

Indeed, something *was* happening with these people: buildings shook, they were filled with the Holy Spirit, they saw visions, experienced being in a trance, heard people speaking in tongues, saw Jesus and heard his voice, received directions in a vision on where to preach the gospel next, and so on. They were encountering the risen Jesus Christ through the action of the Holy Spirit. These experiences were real. No matter how unusual they were, the apostles seemed to accept them as a normal part of their new life in Christ.

The stories were told in a matter-of-fact kind of way. There was no excessive focus on the experiences. The apostles didn't resist them, nor did they seem to seek after the experiences for their own sake. Yet they lived with a kind of receptivity and expectation of the Spirit's action among them.

The openness to religious experience is present in the lives of the Church Fathers as well. Hilary of Poitiers (c. 315-367) speaks of the experience of the Holy Spirit: "Among us there is no one who, from time to time, does not feel the gift of the grace of the Spirit."[3] In another place he describes the experience of being empowered by the Holy Spirit with charisms, saying, "We begin to have insight into the mysteries of faith, we are able to prophecy and speak with wisdom. We become steadfast in hope and receive the gifts of healing."

St. Augustine (c. 354–430) described the experience of his own conversion in great detail:

So was I speaking and weeping in the most bitter contrition of my heart, when, lo! I heard from a neighboring house a voice, as of boy or girl, I know not, chanting, and oft repeating, "Take up and read; Take up and read." Instantly, my countenance altered, I began to think most intently whether children were wont in any kind of play to sing such words: nor could I remember ever to have heard the like. So checking the torrent of my tears, I arose; interpreting it to be no other than a command from God to open the book, and read the first chapter I should find.... I seized, opened, and in silence read that section on which my eyes fell: Not in rioting and drunkenness, not in chambering or wantonness, not in strife and envying; but put ye on the Lord Jesus Christ, and make no provision for the flesh, in concupiscence. No further would I read; nor needed I: for instantly at the end of this sentence, by a light as it were of serenity infused in my heart, all the darkness of doubt vanished away.[4]

In the midst of a deep outpouring of emotion, this towering intellect, St. Augustine, heard a voice, a voice of a child, no less. He didn't know who the child was or where the voice was coming from, yet he felt compelled to listen to the voice. He obeyed. He read the first passage he opened to. The words instantly penetrated his heart; the words came alive for him and he experienced a touch of the Holy Spirit that freed him from doubt and changed his life forever. It is not an exaggeration to say that this great philosopher, who had sought the truth for so long and who had battled with the weakness of his own flesh at such a deep level, was changed in an instant. The experience of God, the touch of the Holy Spirit, became the foundation of a whole new life for him.

These stories make clear that at the heart of this religious experience is a new knowledge, an experiential knowledge of God in the Holy Spirit. This isn't just head knowledge, that is, the acquiring of facts about God, but it's knowing in the biblical sense. This means, "to experience him, to enter into a personal relationship with him, interacting with him and letting oneself be acted upon by him: 'now that you have come to know God, or rather to be known by God' says Paul (Gal 4:9); in heaven 'then I shall know fully, even as I have been fully known' (1 Cor 13:12)."[5]

It's important to see that the willingness to let "oneself be acted upon" by God is a fundamental aspect of coming to a genuine or fuller knowledge of him. The Holy Father, Pope John Paul II, has made this aspect of receptivity to God's action, which he describes as being "docile to the working Holy Spirit," a central piece of his pastoral strategy for the whole Church.[6] Pointing to the teaching of the Second Vatican Council he said, "The Council, then, makes an earnest plea in the Lord's name that all lay people give a glad, generous, and prompt response to the impulse of the Holy Spirit and to the voice of Christ, who is giving them an especially urgent invitation at this moment."[7]

Pope John Paul II is essentially saying that not only he, but the bishops of the world are calling upon every baptized Catholic to do exactly what St. Augustine did: give a "glad, generous, and prompt response to the impulse of the Holy Spirit." He is calling us to be open to genuine religious experience. St. Bernard of Clairvaux gave the same exhortation nearly a millennium ago, "Let those without experience burn with desire so that they will not so much know as experience."[8]

The openness to the experience of God is a fundamental characteristic of all the saints. The saints are men and women who encountered God. They knew him by way of personal experience. That experience produced within each of them a deep conviction that Jesus was alive and acting in the present. Again, Pope John Paul II stated that the apostles, and along with them, the entire Church, lives with the "certainty that Jesus Christ is alive, is working in the present and changes lives."[9]

What I find curious is that we as Catholics, more than almost any other Christians, live with a reverence for the saints. We read about their lives, we celebrate their feast days, and we are regularly exhorted to imitate them with our own lives. As we seek to do that we typically focus our attention on the good works and the asceticism, or the spiritual disciplines they practiced. We focus on the externals—the fasting, almsgiving, and practices of self-denial, and the long hours of prayer that were an important part of their lives. Yet we tend to overlook the experiential dimensions of their life as disciples. We expect to go through all the hardships and self-denial the saints show us, but we almost never expect to encounter the Lord Jesus the way they did. The irony is that without that personal, experiential knowledge of God, the saints would not have been able to live the heroic love we seek to imitate.

Mother Teresa gives us another more contemporary example of this very point. In recent months the Missionaries of Charity have made public for the first time certain details about Mother Teresa's spiritual journey. Those who were publishing the details about Mother Teresa's personal spiritual life said, "It would be hard to understand Mother Teresa of Calcutta's work without being aware of the mystical experiences she had, which were the origin and foundation of the Missionaries of Charity, and impelled her to don a sari and go out into the streets to care for the poorest of the poor."[10]

The same thing can be said of nearly—or quite possibly—all the saints. The personal experience of the Lord Jesus Christ in the power of the Holy Spirit is the "origin and foundation" of all the heroic work of the saints. It allowed them to see what the Lord was calling them to and it released the dynamism and power they needed to fulfill that call.

Like all of us, Mother Teresa struggled to hear the Lord, and to know his will for her life. The published excerpt taken from a letter Mother Teresa gave to her spiritual director records a conversation she had with Jesus. Because the letter is so instructive and inspiring I will include parts of it here:

"At that time, Mother Teresa worked in Calcutta, India, as a religious of the Sisters of Loreto. During her prayer, Christ asked her to go out into the streets and proclaim him among the abandoned of India, especially girls.

"How could I?" she wrote. "I have been and am very happy as a Loreto nun. To leave that what I love and to expose myself to new labors and suffering, which will be great, to the laughingstock of so many, especially religious, to cling and choose deliberately the hard things of an Indian life, to loneliness and ignominy, to uncertainty? And all because Jesus wants it, because something is calling me to leave all and gather the few to live His life, to do His work in India."

"In her prayers, particularly her Communions, Jesus constantly asked her, 'Wilt thou refuse? When there was a question of thy soul I did not think of Myself but gave Myself freely for thee on the Cross and now, what about thee? Wilt thou refuse? I want Indian nuns, victims of my love.'" Mother Teresa explained all this in a letter to her spiritual director and to the archbishop.

"My own Jesus, what you ask is beyond me," the then Sister Mary Teresa responded. "I can hardly understand half of the things you want. I am unworthy. I am sinful. I am weak. Go, Jesus, and find a more worthy soul, a more generous one."

Christ said to her, "No—your vocation is to love and suffer and save souls and by taking the step you will fulfill My Heart's desire for you. You will dress in simple Indian clothes or rather like My Mother dressed, simple and poor. Your present habit is holy because it is My symbol. Your sari will become holy because it will be My symbol."

"Jesus, my own Jesus, I am only Thine," the nun answered. "I am so stupid. I do not know what to say, but do with me whatever you wish, as you wish, as long as you wish. I love You not for what You give, but for what You take ... don't allow me to be deceived, I am so afraid ..."

Christ calmed her by describing what the future would be like: "I want Indian nuns, Missionaries of Charity, who would be my fire of love amongst the poor, the sick, the dying, and the little children.... Little one, give Me souls," Jesus insisted, according to the nun. "Give Me souls of the poor little street children. How it hurts, if you only knew, to see these poor children soiled with sin. I long for the purity of their love. If you would only answer and bring Me these souls. Draw them away from the hands of the evil one. If you only knew how many little ones fall into sin everyday. There are plenty of nuns to look after the rich and the well-to-do people, but for My very poor, there are absolutely none. For them I long, them I love. Wilt thou refuse?"

Some weeks went by. Then, on January 6, 1948, Archbishop Perier called Mother Teresa and said: "You may go ahead."[11]

Defining Religious Experience

Mother Teresa's personal encounter with Jesus provides a vivid example of the reality of religious experience. She lived in a conversation with Jesus, one that touched her whole person. And it was that very experience that gave her the courage, the faith, and the love she needed to begin the Missionaries of Charity. Nothing else would have done it for her. She needed to know Jesus' will; she needed to experience the convincing power of his own voice. Though, by God's providence, she lived most of her years as a Missionary of Charity in the Dark Night, it was the experiential knowledge of Jesus' words to her that became the foundation of all her future work.

Mother Teresa's story provides a kind of paradigm of the characteristic elements of religious experience. Defining religious experience is complicated and fraught with difficulties. An exhaustive definition of religious experience is beyond the scope of this book. Luke Timothy Johnson provides an operational definition in his study of religious experience that can help us lay hold of its basic elements. He defines it this way: "Religious experience is a response to that which is perceived as ultimate, involving the whole person, characterized by a peculiar intensity, and issues in action."[12]

The elements of his definition perfectly fit the account of Mother Teresa's experience of Jesus' call to her. First, she was responding to Jesus, the one whom she "perceived as ultimate," who was calling out to her. The experience touched her whole person, her mind, emotions, will, and memory with a peculiar intensity. It surfaced her deeply held personal fears, her self-doubt, as well as her passionate love for Jesus. The encounter brought her to tears and made her angry; it stirred in her a new level of courage and missionary dynamism. Finally, it moved her to action, to do something she was convinced she didn't have the power to do. The personal experience of Jesus' action in her life changed her, making her capable of responding to Jesus' will for her. Once she confirmed through a process of discernment that indeed it was Jesus whom she was encountering, the experience of his power and presence provided the confidence she needed to risk everything, to leave the security of her former religious life and to place all her trust in Jesus' words to her.

Mother Teresa's story is mirrored in the lives of all the saints. It is not because they were "special" or different than you and I, but because it is a fundamental part of the normal Christian life. The way each of the saints encountered Jesus, the particular details and intensity of the experience, as well as the nature of his call, was unique to each of them. What was common to them all was the reality of the personal, life-changing experience of Jesus' presence and power. They didn't experience Jesus because they were saints, but because they were disciples, men and women touched by the waters of baptism who had been given the gift of the Holy Spirit.

The saints had a living experience of the very same reality Jesus spoke about in the Gospel of Luke, when, at the beginning of his public ministry he stood up before his brethren in the synagogue in Nazareth and said: "The Spirit of the Lord is upon me, because he has anointed me to preach good news to the poor. He has sent me to proclaim release to the captives and recovering of sight to the blind, to set at liberty those who are oppressed, to proclaim the acceptable year of the Lord" (Lk 4:18-19). Jesus provides for us here the true paradigm of religious experience. He himself had encountered the power of the Holy Spirit in a new way, that same Spirit he had known for all eternity. It was the Holy Spirit who was to lead and empower the ministry of Jesus of Nazareth.

Pope John Paul II has reminded all of us on many occasions that we share in the same spiritual "anointing" that Jesus proclaimed that day in Nazareth: "With this spiritual 'unction,' Christians can repeat in an individual way the words of Jesus: 'The Spirit of the Lord is upon me ...'"[13] Every disciple can and should say these words, which are more than mere words. They are the proclamation of a fact, of what should be a life-changing, personal encounter with the risen Jesus Christ. This is to be the foundation of every single Christian life. It is not a reality exclusive to the saints; they didn't receive this because they had somehow reached the appropriate level of holiness to merit Jesus' personal attention. Rather, it was the very experience of Jesus' personal love and power in their lives, some who at the point of encounter were living lives steeped in sin, which gave them what they needed to become saints. Religious experience, that is, experience of Jesus Christ in the power of the Holy Spirit was the starting point, not the end point.

Christian Religious Experience Is Unique

Johnson's operational definition of religious experience is helpful, but it's one that is not exclusive to the Christian experience. It's a definition that could be applied to a "New-Ager," a Mooney, or even a Satanist. We're living at a time in history when religious experience of all kinds has become commonplace. The wide-spread secularization of culture, with its intensely pluralistic and consumerist character, coupled with the collapse of a distinctively Christian culture, has created a spiritual vacuum. Counterfeit spiritualities of all kinds have emerged to fill the void and to feed people's hunger for transcendent meaning. Religious experience has become another commodity. Fortune-tellers, palm readers, herbalists, psychics, New-Agers are marketing their wares, promising inner harmony and a means to get in touch with the "energy" people need to fill their spiritual void.

My intention in this chapter has been to reaffirm the reality of Christian experience and not simply religious experience as such. There is a distinct difference between Christian religious experience and the kind of plurality of religious experiences emerging throughout our culture. The focus for the "new spiritualities" is not on the object of the religious experience, that is, the source of the energy or power behind the experience, but it's on the experience itself. Typically the focus of the "experience" is oneself, one's inner states. The goal is to find a kind of inner harmony or touch a power that is within me, that I am said to possess but that is for various reasons being blocked by negative ways of thinking or feeling. The role of the gurus or masters is to help remove the blocks that are holding back the release of that interior energy or force.

Gary Zukav's book, *The Seat of the Soul,* a New York Times bestseller, is typical of the popular "new spiritualities." The back cover of the book provides an insight into Zukav's particular twist on religious experience: "*The Seat of the Soul* is about the birth of a new species—and the explosion of human perception past the five senses.... It is about authentic power—the alignment of personality with the soul ... it's written for the largest, fastest-growing market the world has ever seen or ever will see. That is because the new species is being born inside of us."

Zukav speaks of "an emerging force" that is unfolding a "great vision" for everyone. He says, "Humanity, the human species, is longing now to touch that force, to shed that which interferes with clear contact." He claims that "in this hour of human evolution" it's time to "transcend religiosity and spirituality and assume the position of authentic power that is longing to be born."[14] His basic point is that there is an evolutionary force at work in all of us attempting to take us to a new level of knowing—beyond the five senses.

This kind of "new spirituality" is enormously popular today. It fits the demands of our secular culture, with its emphasis on pluralism, tolerance, and above all, its absolute certainty that all truth is relative. It provides the alternative to traditional religion, which is seen as intolerant and absolutist, promoting the very kind of "religiosity" Zukav is seeking to "transcend."

Unfortunately, many baptized Catholics are embracing this kind of "spirituality" because it allows them to fit more harmoniously into our secularized, pluralistic culture, and it gives them some feeling of religious experience. The lack of an authentic Catholic formation and in many cases, the absence of any genuine Christian religious experience leaves far too many Catholics vulnerable to this.

The Christian understanding of religious experience is quite different than this. As one author put it, "For the Bible, a separation between the objective content of divine revelation and the subjective experience of a Christian is unthinkable. Throughout scripture, particularly in the writings of St. Paul and St. John, we see that Christian experience in its most authentic sense is intentional; that is, it is experience of the mysteries of the faith, it is not merely a psychological phenomenon which can be attributed to any of various causes."[15] The word "intentional" here is being used in the philosophical sense of being "about" something else.

What are the "mysteries of the faith" that are the object of authentic Christian experience? First, it's the experience of a person, of Jesus Christ, true God and true man, not the experience of some vague force or psychic phenomenon. The power and dynamism of Christian experience is the result of coming in living contact with the risen Jesus Christ in the power of the Holy Spirit. That contact happens primarily, but not exclusively, through the sacraments. It also comes through the preaching of the gospel, through the experience of charisms, through signs and wonders, and the many and varied ways the Lord acts among his people.

Christian experience is not simply experience for experience' sake. People who are proponents of the "new spirituality" tell me that for them the goal is not the "object" but the feeling of harmony or energy. Where it comes from or what it means doesn't necessarily interest them. Christian experience, if it is to be authentic, is directed toward *the truth*, not "a truth," or "my truth," but to "the truth." The point is to actually know the truth. It isn't simply to have an experience of power, but rather to know him who is the source of that power. That truth is a person, Jesus Christ, who is the way, the truth, and the life. The goal of the experience is to be conformed to him. Knowing that truth puts one in contact with his life-transforming power. That power produces genuine interior freedom: "you will know the truth, and the truth will make you free." (Jn 8:32)

Conclusion

Religious experience is a fundamental element of the normal Christian life. It is not limited to the "spiritual elite," nor is it to be sought after simply for its own sake. Knowing God through a conscious, personal encounter through Jesus Christ in the power of the Holy Spirit is Christianity. We were made for that encounter. Hans Urs Von Balthasar highlights this astounding fact when he writes, "The vital thing is the living encounter with God who speaks to us in his Word, whose eyes pierce and purify us 'like a flame of fire' (Rv 1:14).... Man was created to be a hearer of the word, and it is in responding to the word that he attains his true dignity. His innermost constitution has been designed for dialogue. His reason is equipped with as much light of its own as it needs to apprehend God speaking to it."[16]

The encounter is irreplaceable. Right doctrine and clear moral principles are necessary, but they are not sufficient. We need more. We are made for more. Faith, if it is living, must have an experiential component. St. Paul said as much, "And I was with you in weakness and in much fear and trembling; and my speech and my message were not in plausible words of wisdom, but *in demonstration of the Spirit and power, that your faith might not rest in the wisdom of men, but in the power of God*" (1 Cor 2:3-5, italics added).

Christian faith is built on "the demonstration of the Spirit and power" and not merely on persuasive argument. What St. Paul is telling us is that Christian faith is the result of God's direct action. He is the one who convinces; he is the teacher; he brings certainty to the mind and heart of the believer.

This is the experience that so many people are searching for in our increasingly secularized culture, yet our society is closed to this encounter with God. God is driven out; he is silenced. Man is left standing alone. The need for a living knowledge of God remains, but since God is no longer welcome, man is left to create counterfeits, substitutes acceptable to the secular culture. Thus we see our culture falling back into various types of paganism, into religious forms that allow man to maintain his "control" over God. Ultimately, these spiritual alternatives cannot satisfy.

The Church today is confronted with a tremendous challenge. She must not only defend her doctrine and creeds against error, but she must provide the place of encounter once again. She must open the door to authentic religious experience, to a living knowledge of God, one rooted in *the demonstration of the Spirit and power.*

FOUR

The Baptism in the Holy Spirit

In the mid-'90s I led a short-term missionary team to Uganda, Africa, for a series of Catholic evangelistic events. Part of the mission had us working in a diocese that was experiencing the beginnings of a genuine spiritual revival. For some time I had heard from friends and missionaries in other parts of Uganda about the wonderful work of evangelization that was occurring in this region of the country. So I was looking forward to taking our teams there to see firsthand what was happening.

The local leaders had planned a two-day evangelistic crusade to be led by our team. The crusade was to build toward a special all-day event to be held on Sunday. The event was the elevation of the local diocese and its bishop to an archdiocesan see. Becoming an archdiocese was a great event and the whole region was caught up in the celebration.

The installation took place in a large open field with nearly twenty-five thousand people in attendance. The five-hour ceremony was a joyful celebration of faith and it was a privilege for our team to be able to participate in it. The beautiful colors, the tribal dance, and the rich native symbols moved all of us. But what stirred me the most was the vibrant faith and the genuine fervor of the people. The Church there seemed so young and alive compared to the Church in the West. People danced and sang with all their energy—including the clergy.

I commented to one of the local priests how striking it was to see so much dynamic faith and genuine hunger for God. He said that part of what we were seeing was the excitement building toward the installation, but the primary reason for it was the "revival" they had been experiencing in the region. He said that in the previous two years thousands of people from the local villages had come to the faith. These were people who for the most part were members of various tribal religions and who had never been baptized.

When I asked him how the "revival" began, he pointed to a tall priest who was standing near the stage and said, "ask Fr. Paul, he'll tell you." This priest had been instrumental in leading the evangelistic efforts from which the revival emerged.

When the installation finished I approached Fr. Paul and introduced myself. I asked him if he could tell me the story behind the harvest they were experiencing. He said I needed to hear "the story behind the story." So we hopped in his beat-up old jeep and made our way back to the hotel where our team was staying.

He began by telling me that his real name wasn't Fr. Paul, but that his friends called him that because of the conversion experience he had just two years earlier. The Lord had "knocked him down," just like he had done to St. Paul.

He continued, "I was ordained a priest ten years ago. For two years things worked OK, but then I began to lose my faith. I became angry and very worldly. I drank too much and violated my vow of celibacy many times. I wasn't happy, so I decided to leave the priesthood. I was an ambitious guy and I knew I could influence people so I decided to get involved in politics. I had heard about a retreat for lay leaders that was happening at a place called the Emmaus Center in another part of Uganda." (I knew of the Center he was speaking about because we had collaborated with them over the years in leading retreats like the one he mentioned.)

His reason for attending the retreat was, as he said, "to shake hands." He saw an opportunity there to meet influential lay people who could eventually help him pursue his political ambitions. When he arrived at the Center he took an open seat near the front. The first talk, which was given by a young layman, had already started. The theme of the talk was repentance and conversion. The young man used part of the talk to give his own testimony, which included an open, honest account of his willful resistance to God's call in his life.

About halfway through the talk, as the young man began to present the basic elements of the gospel, Fr. Paul began to experience something totally new. He said, "As the young man was preaching I felt a strange sensation; my whole body felt very warm and I began to tremble slightly. Then I had an overwhelming sense of the presence of the Lord. It seemed as though the Lord was coming toward me. The closer he came the more my body trembled. The young man was still speaking, but I was so caught up in what I was experiencing that I didn't even notice what else was going on around me. As the Lord drew near I became very conscious of my sin; it felt like a physical weight pressing down on me. It became so intense I literally fell to the ground. The weight on me was so heavy I couldn't move. Then I heard the Lord say, 'repent!'

"When I heard those words, I was filled with the fear of God. All my sins flashed before me. I felt a profound conviction for my sin; I saw how dark it was. Then, spontaneously, I began to repent, out loud, in front of all these strangers. Laying there, flat on my back I shouted out every sin that flashed before me. I didn't care who heard what, I just wanted to get it out of me. I felt so much sorrow I began to weep for my sin in way I had never done before.

"As I wept I felt cleansed and all the weight of my sin lifted. Then I felt a tidal wave of love and mercy sweep over me. My heart filled up with an awareness of Jesus' love for me. I knew he was there with me, touching me, giving me the power to be free from all the sin in my life. The tears of sorrow turned to tears of joy. I was so happy I wanted to dance, but I still couldn't get up.

"Then the last thing that happened in the whole experience was a new commission from the Lord. I sensed him saying to me that he had called me to be a priest, and that he had anointed me to preach the gospel to the poor. He told me he was giving me a second chance. At that moment I knew without a doubt what I was called to do. Then I stood up, raised my hands in the air and began to praise and thank the Lord for his mercy. Everybody around me was doing the same thing. As I praised him I felt a new power, a new freedom within me. I prayed in tongues for the first time. It was an unforgettable experience. And that's why everyone who knows the story calls me Fr. Paul."

That was just the beginning of the story. From that day on everything changed for Fr. Paul. He returned home after the retreat and told his priest friends about what had happened to him. They were both shocked and delighted by the news. He described to me the concrete changes he experienced over the next few months. He had a new passion to read Scripture, his prayer life came alive after years of little or no personal prayer, he had fresh ideas and energy for ministry, and most of all, he experienced a new level of self-control.

Within just a few months time Fr. Paul felt the Lord tell him to begin preaching in the remote villages of the diocese. With the help of fellow priests and some of the laymen from the Emmaus Center, he went out to as many villages as he could. The team preached the gospel and he told his story over and over again. People in every village began to respond to their message. They weren't quite ready to provide the teaching and formation for the number of people who responded, so they raised up more mission teams who could bring a large number of people through the initiations process into the life of the Church.

Something Is Happening

Fr. Paul's story is an amazing one. It's the kind of story you expect to find in the Acts of the Apostles. Though the dramatic nature and the Pauline quality of his experience are atypical, the essential elements of his encounter with the Lord are not as rare as one might think. His story provides a dramatic example of a type of religious experience that has reemerged in the Church on a broad scale since the Second Vatican Council. The experience is called the baptism in the Holy Spirit. This experience is at the heart of the worldwide movement called the "charismatic renewal." The movement, which is less than forty years old, has been identified by Pope John Paul II as an "eloquent manifestation" of the Holy Spirit's presence in our day, "a particular gift of the Holy Spirit to the Church," and "a bold statement of what 'the Spirit is saying to the churches.'"[1]

The history of the charismatic movement has been well documented. Though it has taken on various forms of institutional expression, the fundamental purpose of the movement remains the ongoing proclamation and promotion of the experience of the baptism in the Holy Spirit. The charismatic renewal is unlike any other movement in the Church today, if for no other reason than its sheer magnitude. In just thirty-five years nearly 140 million Catholics in 238 countries have been touched by this grace.[2]

From its conception the charismatic renewal in the Catholic Church has had a strong ecumenical quality. The experience of the baptism in the Holy Spirit has touched nearly every Christian denomination. When combined with the Pentecostal, mainline Protestant, Orthodox, Anglican churches and the fast-growing independent neocharismatic churches, the experience of the baptism in the Holy Spirit has touched the lives of nearly 500 million people worldwide. People from every race, every strata of society, clergy, religious and laity, young and old have been touched by this grace.

Clearly something is happening on the level of religious experience. Why is it occurring in our time? What does it mean? What is the Spirit saying to the churches through it? To answer these and other questions we must first look more closely at the phenomenon of the baptism in the Holy Spirit itself. What exactly is it?

Fr. Francis Martin, a biblical scholar and longtime leader in the charismatic renewal, provides a helpful definition: "Baptism in the Holy Spirit is a revelation made to the spirit of the believer by the Holy Spirit bringing about an encounter with the Living Christ and disposing the believer to be ever more docile to the action of the Holy Spirit. As such the grace completes sacramental baptism providing that experiential basis which enables the Christian to enter more personally into a relation with Jesus Christ and with other believers...."[3]

The Holy Spirit begins with God's action. He takes the initiative. It isn't something we stir up through our own resources, through a series of meditations or mantras. It's not simply a matter of connecting with a force or energy within.

At the heart of the encounter with the Holy Spirit is a revelation. The Spirit acts to impart to the believer the kind of experiential knowledge discussed in the last chapter. The knowledge is an experience of the reality of the lordship of Jesus Christ. Fr. Paul's story provides a vivid account of the nature of this revelation of the Holy Spirit. The Holy Spirit acted in such a way as to make the Risen Christ present to Fr. Paul in an entirely new way. Though Christ was present to Fr. Paul in an even more profound way through the Holy Eucharist, he could not see it. In a way, Fr. Paul was given new eyes to see. Through the grace of the baptism in the Holy Spirit he was made capable of seeing something that flesh and blood could not reveal to him.

St. Paul prayed for this very revelation to be given to the members of the church at Ephesus: "I do not cease to give thanks for you, remembering you in my prayers, that the God of our Lord Jesus Christ, the Father of glory, *may give you a spirit of wisdom and of revelation in the knowledge of him, having the eyes of your hearts enlightened,* that you may know what is the hope to which he has called you" (Eph 1:16-18, italics added). At the heart of the baptism in the Holy Spirit is a "revelation in the knowledge of him."

This knowledge can only come from God. It is not the result of study or a fertile imagination. It is a communication to the spirit of the believer from the Holy Spirit. The knowledge given is like a light shining in the darkness. Because our minds are darkened by sin we are not able to come to this knowledge on our own resources. We need God's help to be able to see who Jesus is and what it means for our own lives.

In St. Paul's second letter to the Corinthians he provides a vivid description of the interior battle between darkness and light in the heart and mind of a person, and how the Holy Spirit makes it possible to see the truth about the Lordship of Jesus. He said, "even if our gospel is veiled, it is veiled only to those who are perishing. In their case the god of this world has blinded the minds of the unbelievers, to keep them from seeing the light of the glory of Christ, who is the likeness of God. For what we preach is not ourselves, but Jesus Christ as Lord, with ourselves as your servants for Jesus' sake. For it is the God who said, *"Let light shine out of darkness," who has shone in our hearts to give the light of the knowledge of the glory of God in the face of Christ"* (2 Cor 4:3-6, italics added).

St. Paul makes it clear that God makes it possible for a person to recognize the reality of the lordship of Jesus Christ. God acts by shining his light into the human heart and in so doing dispels the darkness and reveals the divine glory and majesty that shines on the face of the Risen Christ. The darkness is the inability to see clearly who Jesus is. It's the strategy of the devil, the god of this world, to veil the eyes of men so that they cannot see the reality of who Jesus is.

Through the baptism in the Holy Spirit a person experiences this divine initiative in a personal way. God, the Holy Spirit, is acting in a way that touches the whole person. What is communicated is more than information; rather the knowledge is direct contact with the Lord Jesus in the power of the Holy Spirit. In the most intimate way Jesus touches the spirit of the believer. The personal touch is experienced as a release of new power. To draw near to Jesus is to draw near to life-transforming power. He possesses in his person, "all authority in heaven and on earth" (Mt 28:18) and he has been "given ... power over all flesh" (Jn 17:2). The baptism in the Holy Spirit is a direct, personal experience of that power and authority.

"Docile to the Action of the Holy Spirit"

The baptism in the Holy Spirit also disposes "the believer to be ever more docile to the action of the Holy Spirit." It brings about the rediscovery of the presence and power of the Holy Spirit in people's lives. It introduces them to a new relationship with the Holy Spirit, one that is characterized by a heightened, conscious awareness of the Holy Spirit's abiding presence. This new awareness helps to produce a greater docility or sensitivity to the Spirit's promptings.

To be docile means to be teachable, able to be guided and led by the Spirit. This presupposes a real expectation that the Holy Spirit can and will lead us. Jesus established that expectation in his disciples when he said, "it is to your advantage that I go away, for if I do not go away the Counselor will not come to you; but if I go, I will send him to you.... When the Spirit of truth comes, he will guide you into all the truth" (Jn 16:7, 13). The Holy Spirit has been sent by Jesus to guide each of us. To be led by the Spirit is a defining characteristic of the whole of the Christian life: "For all who are led by the Spirit of God are sons of God" (Rom 8:14).

The Holy Father shared a poignant story about how he learned to be led by the Spirit in his own life. In a meeting with international leaders of the renewal gathered in Rome he said, "I have always belonged to this renewal in the Holy Spirit. My own experience is very interesting. When I was in school, at the age of twelve or thirteen, sometimes I had difficulties in my studies, in particular in mathematics. My father gave me a book on prayer. He opened it to a page and said to me: 'Here you have the prayer to the Holy Spirit. You must say this prayer every day of your life.' I have remained obedient to this order that my father gave me nearly 50 years ago, which I believe is no little while. This was my first spiritual initiation, so I can understand all the different charisms."[4]

Every baptized believer ought to be able to say like Pope John Paul II, that they too belong to this renewal in the Spirit and understand all the different charisms that the Spirit pours out on his people. This is the inheritance of a disciple, the gift given by Jesus to each person who has entered the waters of baptism. It's a deeply personal relationship with the Holy Spirit, a dynamic living relationship that is rooted in an actual experience of the presence and power of the Holy Spirit; an experience that can be known and affirmed beyond any doubt.

This kind of personal experiential knowledge of the Holy Spirit was the norm in the life of the early Church. The apostles expected everyone who was baptized to come into this relationship with the Spirit. The expectation was clear from the way they spoke to fellow believers. In St. Paul's letter to the Galatians he poses a question to his audience: "Does he who supplies the Spirit to you and works miracles among you do so by works of the law, or by hearing with faith?" (Gal 3:5). St. Paul's question is given in the context of a larger discussion on the relationship between faith and the Law. Did the Galatians come into right relationship with God through the Law or by faith?

The interesting thing to make note of here is that St. Paul's argument is based on the presupposition that the Galatians had a personal experience of the presence and power of the Holy Spirit. The Galatians knew they had received the Holy Spirit and had experienced miracles. The encounter with the Holy Spirit in power was the defining characteristic of their being in right relationship with God. They knew when and how they had received the Holy Spirit. The Holy Spirit came to them through believing what was preached to them; therefore they could conclude that it was faith that put them in right relationship with God.

In chapter nineteen of the Acts of the Apostles, St. Paul encounters some "disciples" at Ephesus:

"'Did you receive the Holy Spirit when you believed?' And they said, 'No, we have never even heard that there is a Holy Spirit.' And he said, 'Into what then were you baptized?' They said, 'Into John's baptism.' And Paul said, 'John baptized with the baptism of repentance, telling the people to believe in the one who was to come after him, that is, Jesus.' On hearing this, they were baptized in the name of the Lord Jesus. And when Paul had laid his hands upon them, the Holy Spirit came on them; and they spoke with tongues and prophesied. There were about twelve of them in all" (Acts 19:2-7).

Here too we can see in St. Paul's question the expectation that every believer ought to have received the gift of the Holy Spirit and that they would know from experience whether or not they had received it. The disciples had only received John's baptism, so St. Paul baptizes them in the name of the Lord Jesus and each of them experiences the presence and power of the Holy Spirit manifested through the charisms of tongues and prophesy.

In the early Church the reality of the presence of the Holy Spirit was an experience before it was a dogma or doctrine. The disciples could be docile to the Spirit, because they knew through experience that the Spirit was present and acting in their lives. For far too many in the Church today, the Spirit is dogma and is yet to become a lived experience.

"Completes Sacramental Baptism ..."

The grace of the baptism in the Holy Spirit is intimately linked to the sacrament of baptism. The whole of the Christian life is built upon this initial sacrament. The *Catechism of the Catholic Church (CCC)* states,

"Holy Baptism is the basis of the whole Christian life, the gateway to life in the Spirit..., and the door which gives access to the other sacraments. Through Baptism we are freed from sin and reborn as sons of God; we become members of Christ, are incorporated into the Church and made sharers in her mission: 'Baptism is the sacrament of regeneration through water and in the word.'"[5]

The grace of the baptism in the Holy Spirit is not a second baptism or a reality distinct from sacramental baptism. It is a fuller appropriation or release of the very gifts received through baptism. To give a precise description of the experience of the baptism in the Holy Spirit in relation to the sacraments is a delicate task. Cardinal Suenens, who played a very important leadership role in nurturing and giving guidance to the charismatic renewal, addressed this challenge:

We are faced with the difficulty of speaking about a new outpouring of the Spirit when we know that the Spirit has already been given to us in sacramental baptism. The "newness" then is a particular quality: we are concerned here with a new coming of the Spirit already present, of an "outpouring" which does not come from the outside, but springs up from within ... as we grope for words we discover how difficult it is to express the inexpressible, especially when we are speaking of the mystery of God's action. Different expressions are being used to define the experience of baptism in the Spirit: the grace of actualizing gifts already received, a release of the Spirit, a manifestation of baptism, a coming to life of the gift of the Spirit received at confirmation, profound receptivity or docility to the Holy Spirit. By whatever name we call it, those who have had this experience speak of it as a very special grace, as a renewal of their spiritual life accompanied by a feeling of peace and joy of a kind hitherto unknown. They esteem this grace as a revitalizing of the sacramental graces they have already received, conferred at baptism, then at confirmation...This Renewal is experienced as a release of the latent potentials of the Spirit whose desire is to lead each one of us to the full realization of our vocation....[6]

We can go back to the description of Fr. Paul's experience from the beginning of this chapter for a vivid example of the effects of this release of the latent potentials of the Spirit. Fr. Paul had received the gift of the Spirit through baptism and confirmation, but for him the dynamism and power of the Spirit was not awakened until his experience at the retreat center. The awakening provided an experiential basis that enabled him to enter more personally into a relationship with Jesus Christ and with other believers. Through this grace of the Spirit Fr. Paul could say, in a way he had never said before, "Jesus Christ has changed my life. I know that I know him."

Is this experience for everyone? Does every Christian need to have the kind of "Pauline awakening" that Fr. Paul had? Obviously not everyone needs to undergo the kind of dramatic experience Fr. Paul encountered. In fact, most people don't. What everyone needs is a conscious, ongoing relationship with Jesus Christ in the power of the Holy Spirit. Every Christian is called to "walk by the Spirit" (Gal 5:16), that is, to live out one's life under the guidance and power of the Holy Spirit. That means walking with a conscious awareness of the Spirit's presence in one's life, and living with an expectation to receive all that God has promised he would do for the believer through the Holy Spirit. Living with that kind of alert, receptive posture toward the Holy Spirit produces change. For some, as in Fr. Paul's case, the change can be sudden and dramatic, for others it is more gradual, but for all, it can and should be an ongoing experience of a life-transforming relationship in the Spirit.

In their important work on the grace of the baptism in the Holy Spirit, Fr. Kilian McDonnell and Fr. George Montague remind us of the kind of change the Scriptures tell us the Spirit intends to produce in the life of every believer:

The effects of this reception of the Spirit are manifold: sanctification (1 Cor 6:11-19); a new and experiential relationship to God by which we cry "Abba, Father" (Gal 4:6; Rom 8:15), and to Jesus whom we proclaim as Lord (1 Cor 12:3); a union with others in the bond of love, walking in the Spirit by the power of the Spirit (Gal 5:25); love, joy, peace and the other fruits of the Spirit (Gal 5:22); a new insight into the mysteries of God (1 Cor 2:9-15); a taste for the word of God (Heb 6:4-5); the courageous boldness to witness even unto death (1 Jn 2:24-27); and gifts of praise, knowledge, prophecy, healing and other charisms of service for the upbuilding of the body of Christ, each according to the measure of Christ's determination (1 Cor 12:7-11; Eph 4:7-16). As these gifts are sought (1 Cor 14:1) and discerned (1 Thes 5:19-21), they empower members to create that communion which the church is meant to be and to proclaim the church's message of love, justice and peace to the world. This life in the Holy Spirit is not, therefore, one spirituality among others in the church. It is the spirituality of the church.

The gift of the Spirit which is God's infinite love (Rom 5:5) can never be totally appropriated, and for that reason it must be sought repeatedly through prayer (Acts 4:23-31; indeed, at times it needs to be stirred up and rekindled (2 Tim 1:6-7). Thus, especially for those who were baptized in infancy, prayer for the fuller release of the Holy Spirit (the more recent popular understanding of the baptism in the Holy Spirit) is a common way of appropriating the grace of Christian initiation. Such is the New Testament pattern and mandate for the life and growth of the church.[7]

Living a life "in the Spirit," walking in docility to the Spirit's promptings, expecting to receive all that God has promised to give to his people through the Holy Spirit, is the normal Christian life. It is not simply for "charismatic types" or the more "experientially inclined," or worse yet, "for those who need more reassurance." It is for all of us.

Something Is Happening Now

We are living at an extraordinary time in the history of the Church. God is pouring out his Spirit in abundance to all who are eager to receive it. We are living at a moment of awakening. Something fundamental is being restored to the Church. The Spirit is breathing new life upon her. The Church is rediscovering something essential to her life. Recent popes have called it the "grace of a New Pentecost." Pentecost is holy fire; it's power from on high; it's God acting to produce change in his people.

Why is this happening now? Because we desperately need it! Pentecost is the only answer the Church has to give to a secularized world. Pentecost is the demonstration of the Spirit in power; it is Christ risen and present among us, changing lives. It is Pentecost that will burn away the spiritual sloth and indifferentism that has gripped so much of the Church in the West. It is the fire of Pentecost alone that can provide the antidote to the aggressive international pagan culture that is emerging in our time. More than anything else, what the Church needs most now is a New Pentecost. This is precisely what the recent popes have prayed for and called us to with passion and intensity:

Renew your wonders in our time, as though for a new Pentecost.[8]

God grant the Lord would still increase this rain of charisms to make the Church fruitful, beautiful, marvelous and capable of inspiring respect, even the attention and the amazement of the profane world, with its tendency toward secularism.[9]

Pope John XXIII

More than once we have asked ourselves what the greatest needs of the Church are ... what is the primary and ultimate need of our beloved and holy Church? We must say it with holy fear because, as you know, this concerns the mystery of the Church, her life: this need is the Spirit...the Church needs her eternal Pentecost; she needs fire in her heart, words on her lips, a glance that is prophetic.[10]

Pope Paul VI

Renew the miracles of the early Christian communities...so that contemporary humanity will believe in Christ, the one Savior of the world.[11]

Be open to Christ, welcome the Spirit, so that a new Pentecost can take place in every community! A new humanity, a joyful one, will arise from your midst; you will again experience the saving power of the Lord and "what was spoken to you by the Lord"will be fulfilled.[12]

Today, I would like to cry out to all of you gathered here in St. Peter's Square and to all Christians: Open yourselves to the gifts of the Spirit! Accept gratefully and obediently the charisms which the Spirit never ceases to bestow on us![13]

Pope John Paul II

We are seeing these prayers fulfilled in abundance in our day. The remaining chapters of this book will be dedicated to reflecting on certain aspects of this New Pentecost. By looking more closely at the kind of change the Spirit is producing in people's lives through this outpouring of the Spirit we may be able to better understand what the Lord is saying to us through it.

FIVE

Knowing Jesus as Lord

No one can say, "Jesus is Lord" except by the Holy Spirit.

During the summer between my junior and senior year in college I roomed with an old high school friend who attended the same Catholic university. He was an academic All-American football player and a lifelong Catholic who, like many other guys our age, kept his Catholicism on the margins of life. He felt some obligation to attend Mass periodically, but to put it mildly, he wasn't ready to get more serious about his faith. He made that perfectly clear to me on a number of occasions.

We shared a small basement apartment just two blocks off campus. It had a strange layout, with two main rooms, a living room and a small kitchen, attached by a wide hallway. Our beds were set up in that hallway with just enough room to walk from the living room to the kitchen.

One evening, just after I had turned out the lights to go to bed, my roommate, Tom, asked me to turn the lights back on. I flipped the light on, we both sat up and he asked me, "Is the devil real?" The question took me by surprise. I remember thinking, "where did that come from?" He had a concerned, serious look on his face, so I knew he really wanted an answer. I said, "Yeah, he's real."

He then looked at me and said, "No, I mean, is he really real? Like does he have the power to mess with your head?" I said, "Yeah, he does. Why?" He responded, "Because I think he's messing with mine." He then went on to tell me that he had been feeling very depressed and that he had even been thinking about suicide. He said he felt this dark-ness around him and that his mind felt like a runaway train. He couldn't stop all the negative thoughts from racing through his mind. Tom said he couldn't trace the thoughts and feelings to any negative thing that happened in his life, so he wondered if he might be under some kind of spiritual attack.

I told him that I didn't know whether it was the devil or not, but that I did know that Scripture warns us directly to "be sober, be watch-ful. Your adversary the devil prowls around like a roaring lion seeking some one to devour" (1 Pt 5:8). He asked me what he could do about it. I said, "The one thing I know for sure is that Jesus is real, he's alive, he's with us, and that he has total power over the devil and all the pow-ers of darkness. He can help us right now if we ask him." With a look of panic in his eyes, Tom looked at me and said, "Let's do it."

I wasn't completely sure what to do, so I just told Tom to sit quietly and try to fix his eyes on Jesus. He sat at the edge of his bed, all two hundred forty pounds of him, with his face in his hands. I reached out and put my hand on his head and began to pray. I remember that moment as if it were yesterday. I simply asked Jesus to send his Holy Spirit to drive away the devil and any powers of darkness that might be hassling Tom. I really didn't know what else to say. I felt a bit over my head, but I knew that the Lord was with us.

I also remember thinking, "man, if our friends—especially Tom's friends—could see us now." There we were, two college guys in our pajamas, crying out to God for help. It was so unusual. I don't recall even saying a mealtime prayer together up to that point in the summer.

After a few minutes of silence I asked Tom if he was experiencing anything. Lifting his head from his hands he looked up at me and said, "Don't you see it? Don't you see the light?" I said, "No, what light are you talking about?"

He said that as I began to pray he felt as though there was a heavy weight on his shoulders and all he could see was a kind of darkness.

But about halfway through the prayer the darkness and weight started to lift and a light began to fill him. As he was describing the experience he got very excited and said, "He's real! Jesus is here with us. I feel like I'm free!"

Without saying another word he jumped up and ran into the living room to a large chest that we used as an end table near our television set. He opened it, dug down to the bottom, and pulled out a Bible. He immediately opened it and began reading aloud passages from the New Testament. He turned from one section to another, each time finding a passage that talked about Jesus. The more he read, the more excited he got. At one point he turned to me, with passion in his eyes, and said, "This is all true, Pete! Jesus is real!"

It's difficult to describe exactly what was happening with us but the more passages Tom read, the more we both experienced the almost tangible presence of the Lord. It was as if he were in the room leading Tom from page to page and confirming the passages with the presence and power of the Spirit. It felt as though we could reach out and touch Jesus.

After some time we both began praising and giving thanks. Tom fell to his knees, spread his arms, and while holding the Bible in his hands, he began to shout the name of Jesus. What a sight that was! This big, thick, aggressive, manly football player, who would have felt uncomfortable with even the slightest expression of spontaneous prayer, was kneeling on the floor of our apartment in his pajamas at 11:30 at night, holding a Bible and shouting prayers of thanksgiving to God.

We continued praying in earnest for some time, when I began to sense the Lord speaking to me. I tried to be as docile to the Spirit as I could. To my surprise I felt clearly as though the Lord was telling me to wash Tom's feet. My first response was, "You want me to do what?" I thought maybe I was getting a bit carried away in the moment. The thought of washing Tom's feet was embarrassing. Yet as I prayed the sense got stronger and stronger.

Convinced it was the Lord, I decided to go for it. So I walked in the kitchen, grabbed a cake pan from the cupboard, filled it with warm water, picked up the dish-towel, and turned toward Tom. He was still kneeling on the floor with his eyes closed. I walked toward him and said, "Hey Tom, the Lord wants me to do something." He opened his eyes and said, "What?" Just then I felt really foolish, standing there with a cake pan filled with warm water. I thought he would think I was a bit over the edge. But I pressed through the embarrassment and said, "Jesus wants me to wash your feet." To my surprise, he said, "great man, let's do it!"

He sat up at the edge of the bed and I knelt down and began to wash his feet. I remember that moment vividly. The contrast of what was happening in each of us couldn't have been more different. I remember blushing as I reached down to grab his very large feet. I felt so stupid. Yet when I looked up at him, he had tears in his eyes. The Lord was touching him through this simple gesture.

When I finished we continued praying. Then, at the same time, Tom and I both knelt down once again. The mood changed in the room. Without speaking, we were simultaneously overcome with a sense of the reality of what Jesus did for us. We were both kneeling, with our face in the carpet, weeping. Tom looked up at me and said, "The cross of Jesus is all that matters. It's the center of everything. Nothing is more important." I was deeply moved by what Tom said because that was exactly what I had been thinking about at that moment. We both knew beyond doubt that the Holy Spirit was there, teaching us, imparting deep faith knowledge, and giving us a glimpse into the truth and meaning of Jesus' death on Mount Calvary. It was an awesome moment for both of us. We were very conscious of our own sin and weakness, and how our response to Jesus' act of love for us was so small in comparison to what he actually deserved. He gave us so much and we had given him so little. After a few moments Tom said, "Pete, Jesus has done it all. He's the most important person that ever lived. He has all power and nothing can stop him. Jesus is the Lord of everything!" For the next few moments, all we could say was, "Jesus is Lord!"

At 1:00 A.M. we decided to call it a night. After a few minutes Tom said, "Hey Pete, turn the light back on. I can't sleep, let's keep praying." I told him I needed to work in the morning but he insisted. I turned on the light and Tom said, "Let's go to the football field on campus and pray!"

Twenty minutes later we were standing on the fifty-yard line of the football stadium, facing the dormitories and praying out loud for every person we knew. We sang songs, we danced, and we prayed under the stars until the sun came up. Shortly after 6:00 A.M., we headed over to morning Mass then returned home and went to bed. What a night!

Jesus Christ is Lord!

The experience Tom and I shared that night was not only a turning point in Tom's life, but it was a teaching moment for me. A fundamental biblical truth came alive in a new way for me. That is that, "no one can say 'Jesus is Lord' except by the Holy Spirit" (1 Cor 12:3).

Of course, anyone can say the words, "Jesus is Lord!" But what St. Paul is referring to here is that to really know the truth of what is being said, the astounding truth that Jesus of Nazareth, Mary's Son, is *the* Risen Lord of all creation, and that all power, glory, and majesty are his forever, can only be known through the direct help of the Holy Spirit. Jesus Christ cannot be known as "Lord" without the help of God.

When Jesus responded to St. Peter's confession that Jesus was, "the Christ, the Son of the Living God," he said, "Blessed are you, Simon Bar-Jona! For flesh and blood has not revealed this to you, but my Father who is in heaven" (Mt 16:17). Peter's confession was based on an interior knowledge, a faith conviction about Jesus that was given to him by God the Father through the Holy Spirit.

St. Paul proclaims this fact in his letters to the Corinthians:

"But we impart a secret and hidden wisdom of God, which God decreed before the ages for our glorification. None of the rulers of this age understood this; for if they had, they would not have crucified the Lord of glory. But, as it is written, 'What no eye has seen, nor ear heard, nor the heart of man conceived, what God has prepared for those who love him,' *God has revealed to us through the Spirit. For the Spirit searches everything, even the depths of God*" (1 Cor 2:7-10, italics added).

"For what we preach is not ourselves, but Jesus Christ as Lord, with ourselves as your servants for Jesus' sake. *For it is the God who said, 'Let light shine out of darkness,' who has shone in our hearts to give the light of the knowledge of the glory of God in the face of Christ*" (2 Cor 4:5-6, italics added).

In order for anyone to know God's plan and purpose set forth in his Son Jesus, that "secret and hidden wisdom of God," that existed for all ages in the "depths of God," it requires an act of God. In other words, God himself wants to teach us who Jesus is. For as St. Paul says, God is the one "who has shone in our hearts," who has given "the light" that makes it possible to see that God's very own glory, his divinity and majesty is revealed "in the face of Christ."

According to St. Paul God has intended to reveal the truth about his Son not by "plausible words of wisdom, but by the demonstration of the Spirit in power." That's why Jesus told his disciples,

"I tell you the truth: it is to your advantage that I go away, for if I do not go away, the Counselor will not come to you; but if I go, I will send him to you. *And when he comes, he will convince the world concerning sin....* When the Spirit of truth comes, *he will guide you into all truth;* for he will not speak on his own authority, but whatever he hears he will speak.... *He will glorify me,* for he will take what is mine and declare it to you" (Jn 16:7-8, 13-14, italics added).

The Spirit is sent to teach us directly about who Jesus is. We cannot see the truth about Jesus with our naked eye; nor can it be known simply through passing on historical data and information about him. The knowledge that God intends to give every person about his Son is the knowledge that comes from faith, and is the result of the Holy Spirit bearing witness to our spirit that all the gospel says about Jesus is true. This knowledge is meant to be personal, experiential and convincing, so that, as St. Paul says, "your faith might not rest in the wisdom of men but in the power of God" (1 Cor 2:5).

The experience Tom and I shared was precisely this. The Holy Spirit was present fulfilling the wonderful promise Jesus made to his disciples,

"And I tell you, Ask, and it will be given you; seek, and you will find; knock, and it will be opened to you. For every one who asks receives, and he who seeks finds, and to him who knocks it will be opened. What father among you, if his son asks for a fish, will instead of a fish give him a serpent; or if he asks for an egg, will give him a scorpion? If you then, who are evil, know how to give good gifts to your children, *how much more will the heavenly Father give the Holy Spirit to those who ask him!*" (Lk 11:9-13)

We were two young college guys, neither theologians nor saints, who simply cried out to the Lord for help in a time of need. I still marvel that the Lord heard our prayer; he came to us, and gave both of us just what we needed. We experienced the Spirit teaching us directly.

The personal encounter with the Holy Spirit as teacher, counselor and advocate is an important dimension of what is being "rediscovered" in our day. Most Catholics understand that the sacraments and the teaching magisterium of the Church are the normal means by which the Holy Spirit guides and empowers his people. But what has too often been forgotten is that the Holy Spirit is not limited to those means. Jesus intends for us to have a much deeper daily intimacy with the Spirit. Each person, through baptism, has literally become a temple of the Holy Spirit, a dwelling place of God: "Do you not know that you are God's temple and that *God's Spirit dwells in you?*" (1 Cor 3:16, italics added). Yes, it's true! God has made our hearts his dwelling place. And from there he wants to lead, guide, comfort, counsel, encourage and teach us. He wants us to know that he is there; he is not far off on a mountain or up in the sky, he has made his home within us.

That is not just a pious thought given for our comfort, but it is a living, life-changing reality. The apostles knew, beyond a doubt, that they had been given more than commandments, or words for comfort; they were given Jesus' own Spirit and it made all the difference in their lives. They expected to be helped, to be taught and to be led by the Spirit and they imparted that expectation to every disciple they were called to lead:

"I write this to you about those who would deceive you; but the anointing which you received from him abides in you, and you have no need that any one should teach you; as his anointing teaches you about everything, and is true, and is no lie, just as it has taught you, abide in him" (1 Jn 2:26-27).

The "anointing" spoken about by St. John is the Spirit. He was telling them plainly, "you have the Spirit in you and the Spirit himself is going to teach you what you need to know." So strong and clear is the abiding presence of the Spirit that St. John went so far as to say, "you have no need of a teacher." The apostle was not saying that there shouldn't be any teachers in the Church, and that each person, because of the presence of the Spirit, ought to be their own teaching magisterium and final arbiter of the truth. After all, St. John knew well that Jesus appointed apostles for the very purpose of passing on the truth of the faith. John himself was teaching through his letters.

John was exhorting his audience to remember the fundamental truth that is so easily forgotten, that the Spirit abides in us and he wants to lead us to the truth. He doesn't want to be forgotten. The Spirit cannot be a silent, hidden, anonymous, or vague presence somewhere within us. The Spirit wants to be known and heard. He has come to "teach us about everything, and is true." He will not lie nor deceive us.

The apostles taught the early Church to be attentive to the Spirit's presence. They consistently reminded them to, "walk by the Spirit," and to be "led by the Spirit" (Gal 5:16, 18). They understood that the heart of what Jesus had given to them was a new life in the Spirit. They were living the promise Jesus had spoken through his prophets centuries before:

"I will sprinkle clean water upon you, and you shall be clean from all your uncleannesses, and from all your idols I will cleanse you. A new heart I will give you, and a *new spirit I will put within you;* and I will take out of your flesh the heart of stone and give you a heart of flesh. *And I will put my spirit within you,* and cause you to walk in my statutes and be careful to observe my ordinances" (Ez 36:25-27, italics added).

This is the promise of the Christian life. It is the inheritance of the disciples of Jesus. Jesus came to make it possible for us to receive his Spirit. The presence of the Spirit within us is like having a new heart. When we "walk in the Spirit" we receive all that Jesus intended us to have. His fundamental intention is to give us a heart that loves what he loves. He came to give us a heart transplant. The Spirit is within us as Jesus' gift to us, to produce in us the kind of heart that makes us capable of living like a child of God; a heart that is passionately set on loving God and neighbor.

Knowing Jesus

For me, the most memorable aspect of the experience of the Spirit that Tom and I shared that night was the extraordinary way the Spirit spoke to us about the person of Jesus. As soon as we began to pray, Tom saw Jesus in a new way. The Spirit began to give him knowledge of the majesty and power of Jesus, and immediately all the darkness and despair that was plaguing him was gone. Just a taste of the light of his glory dispelled the darkness.

Tom had heard the words of the prologue of St. John's Gospel that speak about Jesus, "In him was life, and the life was the light of men. The light shines in the darkness, and the darkness has not overcome it" (Jn 1:4-5). Through the experience of the Spirit's touch, that passage became a reality for Tom. Jesus was not only "the light of men," but he became that light for Tom. Tom could not only say that passage was true, but now he could say in an entirely new way, that it was true for him. He knew that truth in a deeply personal way.

Watching the effect that knowledge had on Tom in the moment was very moving. It was as though the Spirit had tapped into a reservoir or a spring running deep within Tom's heart. The touch of the Spirit produced a spontaneous explosion of joy, gratitude, and praise. The more the Spirit gave Tom conviction about the person of Jesus, the more he wanted to sing and shout about it. All his inhibitions were gone.

Jesus told the Samaritan woman at the well that he would produce a spring of living water in the heart of anyone who cried out to him: "Every one who drinks of this water will thirst again, but whoever drinks of the water that I shall give him will never thirst; the water that I shall give him will become in him a spring of water welling up to eternal life" (Jn 4:13-14). Again, this truth came alive. I saw that spring well up in Tom. In fact, it looked more like a dam bursting than a spring flowing!

The dam burst because the flow of the Spirit had been held back; it had been blocked inside Tom's heart for too long. He had forgotten, or maybe he never really knew, that he was made to live in the joy of the Holy Spirit; he was "destined and appointed to live for the praise of his glory" (Eph 1:12). But lukewarmness, indifference, sin, and living according to the flesh had held back the flow of the Spirit's grace.

I believe that's where many baptized Catholics and Christians are today. They're dammed up. The cares of this world, "the lust of the flesh and the lust of the eyes and the pride of life" (1 Jn 2:16), dominate our horizons. The noise and clamor to possess, to achieve, and to control make it nearly impossible for us to hear the deeper spring of water within. The rich waters of our baptism, left unattended and stopped up by all that we've given ourselves to, can become stagnant.

That night Tom allowed himself to hear the Spirit cry out within him. He experienced the joy of letting go, of letting the dam burst, and allowing the silenced undercurrent of the Spirit's voice to cry out through him. He surrendered to what the Spirit was doing within him. St. Paul tells us that the Spirit cries out, "Abba, Father!" The Spirit is leading us to cry out for our Father; and that cry, "is the Spirit himself bearing witness to our spirit that we are children of God" (Rom 8:15-16). In other words, the Spirit was teaching Tom that he is God's child. That fact, that astounding reality, burst the dam in Tom's heart. Only the Spirit of God can bring that truth to life in our hearts.

The doorway that opens up this truth about our status as children of God is the person of Jesus. The Holy Spirit comes to teach us about Jesus. He wants to reveal "all the riches of assured understanding and the knowledge of God's mystery, of Christ, in whom are hid all the treasures of wisdom and knowledge" (Col 2:2-3). All the treasures of wisdom and knowledge of God, all the truth about God's plan, and the truths about the origin, purpose, and destiny of the human race are hidden in Jesus. Our personal destiny, the "wisdom and knowledge" about our life is made known to us in him.

In Jesus, God the Father, through the Spirit, is answering for us the riddle of our own existence. He answers the great questions: Where have I come from? Why am I here? Where am I going? And he answers them in a way no philosopher or spiritual teacher can. He doesn't offer a glimpse or a part of the answer, nor does he simply shed some light on the road for us, he himself is the entire answer, he himself is the light.

It's this light that the Spirit comes to reveal. The apostles burned with passion to bring this mystery to light through the gospel. They knew that in Jesus the answer to the riddle of human existence had come. He was the treasure that everyone was seeking. They rejoiced because God had chosen to make known "the riches of the glory of this mystery, which is Christ in you, the hope of glory" (Col 1:27) to everyone.

The Crisis of Our Time

Today, the truth about Jesus is under attack. Joseph Cardinal Ratzinger identified the crisis saying, "The central problem of our time is the emptying out of the historical figure of Christ," and in its place we are given "a Jesus to our size, a Jesus possible and comprehensible."[1] What is being emptied out are the "unsearchable riches of Christ" (Eph 3:8). His utter uniqueness, his unparalleled majesty, glory, and divinity are ignored and he is reduced to the status of a wise man or one of history's "most evolved human beings."

Christ is taken down from his throne, so he can be made to fit into the relativistic, secularized mindset that dominates our culture. In this worldview all truth is relative. No one can claim to know a truth that would apply to all people in all situations. Truth is reduced to subjective assertions about what one believes. It is no longer possible to say, "This is the truth," instead, one can only say, since truth is relative, that, "this is my truth," or "that is your truth."

In order for Jesus to fit into this scheme of things all absolute truth, claims about him must be denied. He cannot be "the way, the truth and the life" for the human race, he can only be "a way" who reveals "a truth," and he can only be "the life" for those who want him to be that. In other words, the objective, unchanging reality of the "riches of the glory of this mystery" revealed in Christ, are rich and glorious only if a person decides it is so for him.

This crisis about the objective, unique claims of Jesus runs deep even within the Church in our day. It is not hard to find theologians, priests, or pastors who insist, in the spirit of the age, that Jesus is not the only savior of the world. Instead they passionately affirm there are many roads that lead to God and Jesus just happens to be one of them. To insist that Jesus is the savior of all is considered a form of intolerance, cultural imperialism, or the height of intellectual arrogance. A disturbing number of biblical scholars call into question or deny the miracles performed by Jesus and some, like a priest professor I had in the seminary, go so far as to deny the bodily resurrection of Jesus.

To say that the "emptying of the historical figure of Christ" is the "central problem" of our time is not hyperbole. It's realism. The consequences are more devastating than the horrors of 9/11 or the ongoing conflict in Israel. To reduce the figure of Jesus, to deny who he is and what he has done, is to remove all hope for the human race. Without the whole Christ, the universal, risen Savior of the world, the light of the world goes dim, the shadows gather, and man can no longer see clearly who he is, where he comes from and why he is here. Without Christ, Lord and Savior of all, the world eventually slides back into paganism, into spiritual darkness. This is precisely what we are seeing today throughout the Western world.

Christ provides the one solution to humanity's most intractable problems, the reality of sin and death. These are two things that most people today choose not to look at honestly. But they are inescapable realities, facts of our existence, and the source of all human misery, whether individual or corporate. The Church knows she bears in the good news of Christ's death and resurrection, the only solution to these inevitable problems.

As great as the problems and sufferings of this world are, with its poverty, wars, racial conflicts, and terrorism, no problem is deeper than the problem of sin and death. Wars can be stopped. Poverty can be alleviated. But from death there is no escape. The Christian vision of death's source is clear: "sin came into the world through one man and death through sin, and so death spread to all men because all men sinned" (Rom 5:12). Death is the consequence of sin. Sin produces death.

Death casts its shadow over man's entire horizon. Some people today want to argue that death is simply natural, the next step in the great evolutionary cycle. This runs in direct contradiction to man's instincts. John Paul II made this clear in a recent letter to the elderly of the world:

"In our human condition touched by sin, death presents a certain dark side which cannot but bring sadness and fear.... However rationally comprehensible death may be from a biological point of view, it is not possible to experience it as something 'natural'. This would contradict man's deepest instincts. As the Council observed: 'it is in the face of death that the riddle of human existence becomes most acute. Not only is man tormented by pain and by advancing deterioration of his body, but even more so by the dread of perpetual extinction."[2]

The Church bears in her heart the objective solution to this dreadful reality. She knows that Jesus Christ has destroyed the powers of sin and death through his own dying and rising:

"And you, who were dead in trespasses and the uncircumcision of your flesh, God made alive together with him, having forgiven us all our trespasses, having canceled the bond which stood against us with its legal demands; this he set aside, nailing it to the cross. He disarmed the principalities and powers and made a public example of them, triumphing over them in him" (Col 2:13-15).

"He himself bore our sins in his body on the tree, that we might die to sin and live to righteousness. By his wounds you have been healed" (1 Pt 2:24).

"Jesus of Nazareth, a man attested to you by God with mighty works and wonders and signs which God did through him in your midst, as you yourselves know—this Jesus, delivered up according to the definite plan and foreknowledge of God, you crucified and killed by the hands of lawless men. But God raised him up, having loosed the pangs of death, because it was not possible for him to be held by it" (Acts 2:22-24).

The apostles proclaimed the simple truth that in Christ Jesus: "we have passed from death to life" (1 Jn 3:14). They knew that man's fundamental problem, the riddle of his existence, had been answered: "Death is swallowed up in victory" (1 Cor 15:54). The apostles knew that death had been definitively conquered because they saw the risen Christ with their own eyes. Jesus, who they knew was dead, rose again. He passed through death and entered a new type of existence, an existence beyond death, a reality no human being had ever seen before. The bodily resurrection of Jesus of Nazareth became the foundation upon which the whole Christian faith was based.

Indeed the Christian faith stands or falls on the bodily resurrection of Jesus from the dead. As St. Paul states, "if Christ has not been raised, your faith is futile and you are still in your sins" (1 Cor 15:17). If Christ has not been raised, death has the final word. Yet the witness of the apostles makes clear that Jesus bore a life within himself that was stronger than death:

"That which was from the beginning, which we have heard, which we have seen with our eyes, which we have looked upon and touched with our hands, concerning the word of life—the life was made manifest, and we saw it, and testify to it, and proclaim to you the eternal life which was with the Father and was made manifest to us—that which we have seen and heard we proclaim to you" (1 Jn 1:1-3).

The apostles realized that "eternal life" had come in the person of Jesus of Nazareth. Jesus bore in his own humanity the one reality that was stronger than sin and death, namely, God's own life. Here we touch on the heart of what St. Paul described as the "mystery hidden for ages but now made manifest." That mystery is a "new creation" (2 Cor 5:17); a new humanity brought into being in the person of Jesus of Nazareth. Jesus did not come simply to better or further our existence here on earth, but instead he came that a whole new existence could be born in him.

This new way of being is life beyond death, a life empowered by the risen Jesus who is no longer subject to death: "for we know that Christ being raised from the dead will never die again; death no longer has dominion over him" (Rom 6:9). The Church now proclaims the fact that the Christian life is an actual sharing in Jesus' risen state. The gospel, which she proclaims to the world, is an invitation to enter the new humanity in Jesus:

"As Christ has been raised from the dead by the glory of the Father, we too might walk in newness of life" (Rom 6:4).

"If the Spirit of him who raised Jesus from the dead dwells in you, he who raised Christ Jesus from the dead will give life to your mortal bodies also through his Spirit which dwells in you" (Rom 8:11).

"Christ's Resurrection—and the risen Christ himself—is the principle and source of our future resurrection: 'Christ has been raised from the dead, the first fruits of those who have fallen asleep.... For as in Adam all die, so also in Christ shall all be made alive.'"[3]

If the Church loses sight of the fact of Jesus' bodily resurrection, his victory over sin and death, and the establishment of the new creation in him, she has nothing to say to the world. The Church doesn't exist primarily to relieve the world of physical suffering, or to cushion the blow of this world's many hardships. Instead, her purpose is to free man from ultimate despair and from the hopelessness that comes from knowing all our strivings are futile, and are swallowed up in the darkness of death. To "empty the historical figure of Jesus" in any way is to rob the world of its only hope and to reduce the Church to the very condition Jesus had warned his apostles about, namely, that of a salt which has gone flat. A condition, which he reminds us, "is no longer good for anything except to be thrown out and trodden under foot by men" (Mt 5:13).

This is the situation the Church finds herself in today: a mortal struggle with the spirit of the age for the soul of the Church. Will the Church remain faithful to her Lord, bearing witness to the whole truth about him? Or will she compromise with the spirit of the age, presenting a Christ to their liking, a Christ cast down from his throne?

It's within this historical context that the Holy Spirit is being poured out on the Church anew. The Lord is pouring forth his Spirit in a fresh way to counter this aggressive pagan culture, and the pervasive spiritual skepticism that dominates it. It is no accident that at the heart of this grace is a revelation of the lordship and majesty of Jesus. The Spirit is coming to help the Church in her time of need, to provide the precise antidote to the problem she is facing.

The solution for the Church at this hour is a new Pentecost. It is the Church's unshakeable, convincing knowledge, given by the Holy Spirit, that "Jesus Christ is Lord!" That's the first message revealed in the outpouring of the Spirit in our day. The Church is the hope for the world because she bears in her heart the glorious revelation of the risen humanity of Jesus of Nazareth. The Spirit wants to set the Church's heart aflame with a passion, an unshakeable faith conviction, about the majesty, beauty, and lordship of Jesus Christ. The faith of Pentecost begins there and it produces a living hope and a burning love that cannot be denied.

If we pay attention to the message that is being revealed through this grace of the Spirit, if we respond to it with an open heart and docility of spirit, the Lord will produce in us what we most need to face the challenges of our time. The first lesson the Spirit is teaching us through this Pentecostal grace is that knowing Jesus personally is the starting point and key to everything.

The Doorway to a Changed Life

For Tom, the experience we shared that night became the doorway to a whole new life for him. It ignited a fire in him and gave him a passion for Christ and a sense of direction in his life that he hadn't known before. He began to pray daily, to read the Scriptures, and to attend Mass on almost a daily basis. He began to go to confession with greater frequency and to seek the help of priests and others for discernment and guidance in his life. He changed crowds, partied less, and even began to take his required theology classes more seriously.

The personal experience of the Lord's power at work in him produced a radical reorientation of Tom's priorities. Christ became the center of his life. He gave to God what belonged to him, namely, his heart, his passion, his trust and obedience. Christianity became more than an obligation he was duty-bound to fulfill.

We began to pray together on occasion and I introduced him to some of my friends on campus who were passionate about following Christ. He even spoke to some of his friends on the football team about Jesus and the need to put him at the center of their lives.

Tom really did change. Over the past twenty years, I've seen many people experience the Lord in a similar way. In most of those cases, the experience, though intense and emotional, led to lasting change. I've also heard people, including orthodox Christians, dismiss this kind of experience as emotionalism, implying that the real stuff of discipleship happens apart from religious experience.

No doubt discipleship is perfected on Mount Calvary, but it cannot be forgotten that faith, the kind of faith that provides the strength to begin the ascent up Mount Calvary is born on Mount Tabor. It is born of a vision of the glory and majesty of Jesus of Nazareth.

SIX

Freedom

"Now the Lord is the Spirit, and where the Spirit of the Lord is, there is freedom."

A few years ago I was part of a short-term mission team that led a series of evangelistic rallies in Hungary. One of the rallies was held in a beautiful town called Pecs. We arrived in Pecs by bus, after having traveled some eight hours from the previous day's rally site. The bus ride to Pecs was unlike any other we had experienced.

One of our team members was a gifted lay leader from India named Romeo. It was the first time he had traveled with one of our teams. Early on in the bus ride we took our normal time of prayer together as a team, then began settling in for the long ride ahead. Just as everyone began to get comfortable, Romeo stood up in the front of the bus and said he had something to share. He told us that he had a strong sense that the Lord wanted us to take the remaining six or so hours of our trip to Pecs to intercede and do "spiritual warfare" together for the next day's rally. He said that he felt we would be confronting spiritual strongholds at the rally and that we needed to begin praying for the help of the Holy Spirit to set people free.

We prayed all the way to Pecs. We arrived in the evening and as we were driving through town someone saw the sports arena that was to be the location for the rally. Romeo suggested we stop at the arena and take a few minutes to pray there. The arena was empty but for a few men who were working on last-minute sound checks and setup. We stood in the center of the arena and began to pray. Within just a few moments each of us experienced a tremendous sense of the presence and power of the Holy Spirit. I knew then that Romeo had heard the Lord, that indeed something significant was going to happen the next day.

As we were praying one of the laborers who was working on setup came up to Ralph Martin and asked him for help. He said that he had been actively engaged in the occult for fifty years and that he wanted to be free from it all. Ralph and some of our team members prayed with him. This man's cry for freedom and his childlike hunger for God turned out to be a good indicator of what was to take place at the rally.

The next day we gathered in the morning for the rally. The sports hall was filled with people of all ages. We began the day with a basic presentation of the gospel and a clear proclamation of Jesus' victory over the power of sin and death through the cross. After the talk, as is our custom, we invited people to come forward for prayer. Most of the arena came forward at the invitation with hundreds of people pressing in on our team members for personal prayer.

I was standing on the stage leading the prayer ministry session when I heard a loud shriek. I looked down to the floor where the noise had come from and one of our team members, a man who was veteran of our missionary campaigns, and pound for pound one of the strongest men I know, was waving to me, with a look of panic in his eyes. I went down to see what had happened.

When I approached this team member he said that a young man had just come up for prayer and when he approached, my friend asked him, through a translator, what he would like prayer for. At that moment the young man tried to strike my friend and he let out the blood-curdling shriek that I had heard. When he did so, a strong, foul smell of sulfur filled the air. I could still smell it as I spoke to my friend.

The young man in question was standing just ten feet from my friend as we spoke. I turned to speak with him and what I saw was shocking. He was a young man, probably in his late twenties, wearing a black leather jacket with jet-black hair. He had a wild look in his eyes and was making strange sounds and twitching a great deal. My friend and I approached him with a translator and asked if he would like to receive prayer or to talk with someone. He nodded in the affirmative.

I then told one of our team members to find a priest from our team who could assist us in prayer. We found a priest, but when he came close the young man stared at him with a cold, dead look in his eyes, and the priest actually got a bit frightened and said, "I'm not your man on this one!" He helped us find another priest and we led the young man to a prayer room we had set up in the back of the arena.

After just a few moments with him, I had to return back to the stage, but my friend and the priest later gave a detailed account of their time together. They began by asking him a few questions about himself. It took some time before he would say anything, but eventually his story emerged.

He was baptized Catholic as a baby. His parents were communists and never practiced their faith. He hadn't received any religious instruction as a child. His father was a distant, hard man who offered his son little or no relationship. When he reached his early teen years he and his father argued a great deal. At one point the arguing escalated into a physical fight. Physically bruised and emotionally wounded, the young man ran away from home and began living in the streets.

To survive in the street he became a prostitute. Eventually this led to his becoming a pimp, having forced a number of young street girls to work for him. During this time he also began using and selling drugs of all kinds. The drug culture brought him in contact with the occult where he became a serious practitioner of an unusual form of occultism which included a daily ritual of blaspheming the name of Jesus. Simply put, the young man was shrouded in darkness. He was filled with anger, resentment, and a great deal of pain.

After pulling his story out of him they asked if they could pray with him. He nodded. As they extended their hands toward him, they asked Jesus to send his Spirit to help the young man. As they prayed he began to tremble and shake violently. The more they prayed the more he convulsed. He then became physically sick and fell to the floor, where he ended up lying for nearly an hour, motionless, as though he were passed out or sleeping.

When he woke up, it was clear that something had changed in him. His eyes, his countenance had changed. The cold, dark look in his eyes was gone. The twitching and strange noises he was making had stopped. He wanted to talk. The priest asked him if he would like to confess his sins and receive the sacrament of confession. He was eager to confess, so my friend left the room. The priest heard his confession and welcomed the young man back into the Church.

Later that day, as the rally was drawing to a close, I was once again standing on the stage. At this point the arena was filled with dancing and singing. The thousands of young people who were there had pushed up close to the stage and were raising their hands in song, many were locked together arm in arm, jumping up and down with a radiant joy on their faces. As I looked at them I noticed, standing right in the middle of the kids, the young man who my friend and the priest had prayed for. He was standing, with his arms extended as far as he could stretch them, with his eyes closed, his face turned toward heaven, and an enormous smile on his face. I could tell he was weeping because every thirty seconds he would wipe away the tears that were flooding down his face. He was absolutely radiant. I knew he had met the Lord. The Lord was cleansing him, freeing him from all the bondage of sin, the bitterness, the self-hatred, the pain of rejection; it was all being washed away.

Before the day was over, one of our team members introduced him to local leaders who welcomed him into their fellowship and gave him a place where he could start his life all over again.

You were all called to freedom, brethren (Gal 5:13).

There are 315 men on death row in Luzira Prison in Kampala, Uganda. These men are stuffed into overcrowded cells, which are nothing more than concrete boxes. They have no beds, they have no possessions to speak of; they live in the most dire conditions, waiting. They are waiting for their execution. Nobody knows when it will happen. The decisions are made by the powers that be. One day three years ago, guards entered death row, pulled twenty-seven men from their cells and led them to their execution. The rest simply wait.

Something else is happening on death row in Luzira Prison. These 315 men live in peace; they have become a family. The violence and perversion that is so much a part of the prison systems throughout the world is absent. Instead what one finds there is charity, respect, kindness, a hunger for holiness, and a contagious passion for Jesus Christ.

A number of years ago the warden gave inmates permission to study the Bible and pray together. Members of Prison Fellowship International came to support them, to help lead them into a relationship with Jesus. One by one the inmates began to change. They ministered to one another, bringing the healing power of the Holy Spirit into the hopelessness of their situation. Together they confronted their crimes, they confessed their sins, and they helped one another face the reality of their imminent death.

Death row in Luzira Prison has become a temple of praise. A friend of mine has visited the prison on a number of occasions. He is an international leader in Prison Fellowship. In that capacity he has visited many prisons throughout the world. But as he makes clear, there is no prison quite like Luzira. He told me of a recent visit in which he was able to join the men on death row for their prayer time together. He said they filled the prison with praise; and not only with praise, but with a kind of purity and passion in praise of Jesus that he had never experienced before. He was overcome with emotion, standing amidst these men, sentenced to die, with absolutely nothing in this world, condemned to live out their days in the most hopeless of circumstances, yet they praised the risen Christ with abandon.

My friend asked them, "Is it true that there is no violence here on death row?" The answer he received pierced his heart. They said, "Yes, it is true and the reason it is so, is that Jesus Christ runs this prison!" Even many of the guards and attendants are believers.

How is it possible in an overcrowded prison, in the most dire of living conditions, 315 criminals, murderers, thieves, rapists, robbers, are living in freedom? My friend marvels at the level of consistent virtue and genuine holiness these once-hardened criminals now exhibit in their life together. These are transformed men. They know that justice demands they pay for their crimes. They've helped one another make their peace with that fact. Yet it's not death they wait for. They'll tell you they long to see Jesus. They know they have been forgiven. They know they've been given a kingdom. And through the convincing power of the Holy Spirit they know that they have "been born anew to a living hope through the resurrection of Jesus Christ from the dead, and to an inheritance which is imperishable, undefiled, and unfading" (1 Pt 1:3-4).

These men are a sign of contradiction. They know a freedom, living within that huge cement block they call home, that many people on the outside, living in the halls of splendor, never touch. They know the freedom that comes from Christ.

Living in Freedom

For freedom Christ has set us free; stand fast therefore, and do not submit again to the yoke of slavery (Gal 5:1).

A fundamental characteristic of the Christian life is freedom. The work of the Spirit in our day has helped many people rediscover the fact that Christian freedom is a gift of the Holy Spirit. That is, it is a condition produced in us by the Spirit. The Spirit is given to lead us from a condition of slavery to sin into the "glorious liberty of the children of God" (Rom 8:21). St. Paul warns us that we were all once "slaves of sin" (Rom 6:17) and he makes clear that to remain in the freedom Christ has given to us, we must "stand fast" in its defense.

Sin is a power at work within us. A power that needs to be subdued, and literally to be put to death, or it will produce within us its own characteristic fruit: "while we were living in the flesh, our sinful passions, aroused by the law, were at work in our members to bear fruit for death" (Rom 7:5).

The biblical picture of the struggle against sin is clear. Sin is a perversion of human freedom. It refers not only to a particular sinful act, but also to an interior disposition that is set against God's will and his rightful claim over us. Sin produces death, because it cuts us off from the one true source of life, namely, God. Death in its own turn casts a shadow over the human heart, and darkens our mind, producing fear. The devil manipulates the fear of death in order to enslave us. According to St. Paul, Jesus partook of our flesh, "that through death he might destroy him who has the power of death, that is, the devil, and deliver all those who through fear of death were subject to lifelong bondage" (Heb 2:14-15).

Sin's hold is so deep that even the "Law," that is, the Law of Moses, which God gave for our good, contributes to our slavery: "the very commandment which promised life proved to be death to me" (Rom 7:10). How can God's law, which is "holy and just and good," contribute to this condition of slavery? Paul explains it this way: "sin, finding opportunity in the commandment, wrought in me all kinds of covetousness" (Rom 7:8). Because of the "law of sin" within us, the law of God, which is meant for good, exposes the true condition of our hearts toward God. The commandments of God demand that we love him first, with all our heart, soul, mind, and strength. Yet when we look at our lives in light of that command we know we don't fulfill it.

Instead what we find is "all kinds of covetousness" and self-love.

Paul sees this battle being played out in his own life: "I see in my members another law at war with the law of my mind and making me captive to the law of sin which dwells in my members. Wretched man that I am! Who will deliver me from this body of death?" (Rom 7:23-24).

The human struggle for freedom is a struggle against these forces. It's a struggle we cannot win on our own resources, no matter how hard we strive. Paul reminds us, "we are not contending against flesh and blood," but against "spiritual hosts of wickedness," powers that can only be defeated "in the Lord and in the strength of his might" (Eph 6:12, 10). This struggle is played out in everyone's life. The story of the young Hungarian man provides a vivid, dramatic picture of just how real this struggle is. His story may seem extreme, but the battle he waged is common to us all. From day one it seems he was born into an environment crippled by habit patterns of sin that eventually led to his demise. The lack of faith in his home did not equip him for what he was to face. The battle began with his own father: anger, rage, bitterness, and violence eventually led to a break in the family.

Sin ruptures relationship, it severs and divides, and leads to isolation. The young man roamed the streets alone; he was deeply wounded, lonely, easy prey for "the devil prowls around like a roaring lion, seeking some one to devour" (1 Pt 5:8). Sin drove him to the street and sin sought to keep him there. He was trapped in sin. Sin became his way of life. Each step of the way, as he ran away from the pain of rejection, he moved deeper and deeper into slavery.

When we're trapped in sin, sin seems like the only solution to our problems. How was he to live? Sell his body. How could he make more money? Force others, even more defenseless, to do the same. How could he deal with all the interior pain in his life, the bitterness and self-hatred that were eating away at him? Medicate the pain with drugs. If reality is too painful, escape it, run from it, numb it. What could he do to overcome the feelings of powerlessness and emptiness in his heart? Embrace the occult, spiritual counterfeits, which provide the illusion of transcendence but allow him to remain in the shadows, away from the light that would expose the depth of his condition. Jesus said, "Men loved darkness rather than light, because their deeds were evil. For every one who does evil hates the light, and does not come to the light, lest his deeds should be exposed" (Jn 3:19-20). No one trapped in sin wants to see what kind of mess they've made of their life.

Here he is an eternal creature, created for glory, made for joy and beauty beyond compare; sin has worked its spell on him. He is crippled, diseased, twitching, and hissing like a madman. He is left alone to wander the streets. This is the end the devil desires for each of us. His strategy is to convince us all that our lives are ultimately meaningless. If death has the last word, what are we left with? We are stuck in what many spiritual writers have described as a "closed system." If God does not exist, we are left on our own. Self-preservation becomes the driving force in life. The fear of not having enough, of failing to get my share of the limited resources, makes life a competition. What emerges within me is "all kinds of covetousness" (Rom 7:8).

Life becomes an intense race to have, to control, to possess, and to experience. In this system no one can be trusted. I fear that others are getting ahead. I covet their advantage. I'm plagued and agitated by a nagging discontent. I cannot see my way out, "the God of this world has blinded the minds of unbelievers." Satan has placed a veil over our eyes, making it impossible to see beyond the closed system.

Sin, at its core, is a refusal to acknowledge God. The power of sin within us connives with the devil's strategy to exile God from his creation. And here, according to St. Paul, we touch the heart of the matter: "So they were without excuse; for although they knew God they did not honor him as God or give thanks to him, but they became futile in their thinking and their senseless minds were darkened ... they exchanged the truth of God for a lie and worshiped and served the creature rather than the Creator" (Rom 1:20-21, 25).

Sin ultimately leads to idolatry. Idolatry is the refusal to give to God what belongs to him—our love, trust, obedience, and utter devotion. It's the attempt to find life and ultimate meaning apart from him. If God is not there, we will invest our energy, passion, and trust in something else. We end up relating to contingent, passing realities as if they were ultimate. This for St. Paul is slavery pure and simple. Who is more deceived and enslaved than a man who stakes his life on what is passing? How blind is the man who worships something less than himself?

There is no satisfaction for the human heart apart from God. The attempt to find meaning in what we possess, what we have sought for our self-preservation, does not satisfy. We are left empty. But if God is not there, what else will fill that emptiness but more of the same? Isn't this never-ending drive for satisfaction and contentment the source of the staggering proliferation of addictive and compulsive behaviors so characteristic of our culture?

Breaking Through the Closed System

We are living at a moment of fierce spiritual struggle. The culture of the western world, a culture deeply rooted in a Christian vision of reality, is disappearing. In its place has emerged what Pope John Paul II has called "a culture of death." At the foundation of this "culture of death" is the rejection of God. It is the insistence on a way of life without reference to him. And that, John Paul continually warns the West, necessarily leads to the demise of man.

A great deal of helpful analysis of the "culture of death" has already been written. For our purposes I simply want to point out that the "culture of death" is nothing more than the cultural embodiment of the "closed system." And because it is a way of life, it will produce its own fruit. It will produce, and is producing, the kind of spiritual slavery and idolatry that St. Paul tells us about.

We are witnessing the collapse of the distinctively Christian way of life. Joseph Cardinal Ratzinger, observing the signs of the rapid collapse of a distinctive Christian culture throughout the West, warned the whole Church saying, "We cannot calmly accept the rest of humanity falling back into paganism. We must find the way to take the Gospel, also, to nonbelievers. The Church must tap all her creativity so that the living force of the Gospel will not be extinguished."[1] The further God is pushed to the margins of life, the further our culture will slide into spiritual bondage.

What is needed to break through this closed system? What can the Church offer to man? What is God's solution to our struggle?

C.S. Lewis observed the spiritual dimensions of the battle for culture and he knew instinctively that something more was needed: "you and I have need of the strongest spell that can be found to wake us from the evil enchantment of worldliness which has been laid upon us for nearly 100 years."[2]

Something more is needed. The only solution to this "evil enchantment of worldliness" is the dynamic power of the Holy Spirit. It is the fire of Pentecost. It is the power of the risen Jesus Christ poured into the heart of man that will awaken him from the spiritual torpor of the culture of death.

When the apostle John, who was shepherd of the seven churches of Asia Minor, was confronted with the overwhelming power of the pagan culture of Rome that surrounded them, God provided a solution. These fledgling churches, on their own resources, were no match for the dominant culture they were forced to confront. Their faith stood in direct contradiction to the faith of the empire. The emperor demanded to be worshiped as a divinity; he bore the title "Lord and God." John knew they could not offer worship to the emperor. The refusal meant death for them.

The battle lines were drawn. Would the early Church yield, in fear and a desire for self-preservation, or would they remain faithful to Jesus, and refuse to live by the demands of the "closed system" which sought to destroy them? How did the Lord help John? The solution he gave John is the same answer he offers us today: a revelation of the beauty, power, and majesty of the risen Christ. While John was "in the Spirit on the Lord's Day," he heard a voice speaking to him, he turned and this is what he saw:

"I saw seven golden lampstands, and in the midst of the lampstands one like a son of man, clothed with a long robe and with a golden girdle round his breast; his head and his hair were white as white wool, white as snow; his eyes were like a flame of fire, his feet were like burnished bronze, refined as in a furnace, and his voice was like the sound of many waters; in his right hand he held seven stars, from his mouth issued a sharp two-edged sword, and his face was like the sun shining in full strength.

"When I saw him, I fell at his feet as though dead. But he laid his right hand upon me, saying, 'Fear not, I am the first and the last, and the living one; I died, and behold I am alive for evermore, and I have the keys of Death and Hades'" (Rv 1:12-18).

The revelation of the risen Christ broke the power of the "closed system." John knew, by the grace of the Holy Spirit, that Christ had conquered the powers of darkness; indeed, death itself had been "swallowed up in victory" through his dying and rising. John saw his future revealed in the person of the risen Christ; a future outside the "closed system."

The Holy Spirit reassured John, imparting a dynamic faith and hope, giving him the courage and power he needed to face the darkness and to encourage his brethren. The Lord told him directly, "Do not fear what you are about to suffer. Behold, the devil is about to throw you into prison, that you may be tested.... Be faithful unto death, and I will give you the crown of life" (Rv 2:10).

John knew he wasn't alone. There was a power at work in him that was greater than all the powers of darkness. This is the same reassurance the Lord is bringing his people today.

The young Hungarian who was trapped in sin, bound by fear, and oppressed by guilt and shame, was released from years of bondage in a matter of moments by a revelation of the power and majesty of Jesus. Full healing will likely take years for him, but the essential first step, the breaking of the chains that bound him, the impartation of a living faith and a genuine hope, came to him through a demonstration of the Spirit in power.

In Christ he met a power great enough to dispel his darkness, powerful enough to heal his shame and to forgive his sin. No longer an orphan, he knows by way of experience the truth of St. Paul's words: "For all who are led by the Spirit of God are sons of God. For you did not receive the spirit of slavery to fall back into fear, but you have received the spirit of sonship. When we cry, 'Abba! Father'! it is the Spirit himself bearing witness to our spirit that we are children of God" (Rom 8:14-16).

This is the grace that the Lord in his mercy has poured out upon the earth through his Spirit in this century. It's the only antidote that can break the power of the forces unleashed upon the earth in this culture of death. Nothing else can overcome the alienation, fear, and isolation that characterize this culture. Faith, rooted in an experiential knowledge of Jesus Christ, releases the power needed to overcome the world: "For whatever is born of God overcomes the world; and this is the victory that overcomes the world, our faith" (1 Jn 5:4).

What situation could be more hopeless or desperate than death row in Luzira Prison? These are convicted murderers, rapists, thieves, liars, men bearing diseases, forced to await their death together, in some of the most despicable living conditions one can imagine. Prisons are known to be breeding grounds for violence, dehumanizing, degrading environments that lead men into ever-deeper levels of darkness and despair. Yet in Luzira, light and hope and joy are flowing like water in the desert.

These men have been transformed. They are no longer slaves, but free men. Christ has conquered them, he has subdued the rage, anger, and lust that dominated their lives; he has given them new hearts, enabling them to feel tenderness, love, and mercy toward one another, to bear the fruit of the Spirit.

Awakening the Baptized

By the present action of the Holy Spirit in the lives of these men, the grace of baptism has been awakened. The personal experience of the power of the risen Christ, that revelation from the Spirit of God to the spirit of the believer, provided an experiential basis for the reality of their baptism. Baptism was no longer simply an event hidden somewhere in the past that has no visible, tangible effect in the present.

Through the present action of the Holy Spirit, the reality of what was accomplished in baptism is brought to the forefront. These men now know that their "old self was crucified with [Christ] so that the sinful body might be destroyed," so that they may "no longer be enslaved to sin." They know that they have died with Christ in baptism and that "he who has died is freed from sin" (Rom 6:6-7).

The Spirit brings freedom from sin. We are all called to freedom. Too many men and women who have received the waters of baptism have yet to enter into a living experience of true freedom. They are controlled by habit patterns of sin, dominated by the same rage, anger, greed, lust, fear, and ambition that once controlled the men of Luzira. Despairing for want of real change, they have no earthly idea that they have been given the power in baptism to make a break from the sin that clings so close and to live in the genuine freedom of the sons and daughters of God.

Christian freedom is real; it is not a fantasy. Therefore St. Paul can say with confidence to the Romans and to every baptized person: "Let not sin therefore reign in your mortal bodies, to make you obey their passions. Do not yield your members to sin as instruments of wickedness, but yield yourselves to God as men who have been brought from death to life.... For sin will have no dominion over you!" (Rom 6:12-14).

SEVEN

A New Pentecost

"You shall receive power when the Holy Spirit comes upon you; and you shall be my witnesses ... to the ends of the earth."

Bob studied agronomy—soil science—at Texas A&M University. He married just before starting his M.S. program in soil science. He was an ambitious student, who poured himself into his academic career. While pursuing a Ph.D. he spent day and night studying, researching, writing articles, and, by his own admission, having just enough time at home to get the rest he needed to go back to work.

Bob graduated with honors. He was sought after for teaching posts at Cornell University, Johns Hopkins University, and Iowa State University. He chose Iowa State because of the prestige of the soil science group and the career opportunities it offered. Once he joined the faculty he felt nervous and slightly intimidated. He feared the possibility of failure, of not being able to keep up with the big boys. So, once again he threw himself into his work night and day.

During this time Bob's young family was growing as fast as his career. Just a few months after arriving at Iowa State, Bob and his wife had their second child. Two years later they became the proud parents of twin girls. After the birth of the twins, Bob felt on top of the world. His family was growing and his career was taking off. His research was being published, he won a couple of important awards, rival schools began to offer him teaching positions, and he was given substantial salary incentives to stay at Iowa State. From his vantage point, things couldn't be better. Then the tide began to turn.

Bob received a phone call at work from a local police officer. He told Bob there had been an accident in his home and that he was needed there immediately. Bob rushed home to find out that one of his one-year-old twin girls was fighting for her life. She had fallen into a bucket of water that had been sitting on the basement floor. When she fell in, her head was submerged and the weight of her body prevented her from being able to lift herself up. When Bob's wife found her she was no longer breathing. The ambulance rushed her to the hospital but despite all their efforts they were not able to revive her. Within forty-eight hours of the accident all of her body functions shut down and she died.

Bob and his wife were devastated. They didn't know how to help one another cope with the tragedy. Bob's wife became very quiet and withdrawn. Bob, thinking she just needed space, let her withdraw and he coped by pouring himself back into his career. It was difficult, but in Bob's mind it was something they would get through if he remained strong.

Yet a couple of months later, Bob received another phone call at work. This time it was from his wife. She asked him to come home because she needed to talk. It was the middle of the workday so Bob insisted that they talk over the phone. She told him that she was pregnant and that she did not think Bob was the father. Bob immediately left for home only to find when he arrived that his wife's bags were packed; she had decided to leave him. Bob's world had collapsed.

Bob described his feelings this way, "After she left I remember standing, staring out the back window feeling crushed and empty. All of the things at work that had seemed so important now seemed like nothing in the face of losing my family. I felt a black cloud come into my mind and I basically experienced emotional shock. That night was the longest night of my life. It was as though time itself had slowed down. After I had put the children to bed I had nothing to distract my mind from the pain and anguish I felt. It was as though I could sense each second ticking by, and I had the most out of control, painful, and fearful emotions and thoughts in me. I was tempted to commit suicide that night, but the thought of my daughters sleeping in the adjacent bedrooms gave me the strength to resist the temptation. I did not want my marriage to end. In an effort to gain control of the situation I pursued my wife, trying to convince her to come back home and give our marriage a chance. The harder I pushed the further she went away. Friends of mine encouraged me to open my life to God, but I couldn't hear them; I had my own agenda for how I was going to fix it all. But finally, after some months, my wife decided to file for divorce. I felt completely helpless, like my life was spinning out of control. Once again my friends asked me to open my heart to God. I had nowhere else to go. I decided to give God a chance."

Bob believed that God existed, but at the time he didn't believe in Jesus. He found himself a Bible and began to read it. He said, "I decided that I would read from the Bible and pray each night after my daughters were asleep. I had plenty of time to pray and read; I was so hurt it was difficult to sleep. I began to read the New Testament and the Psalms. The psalms that expressed emotional turmoil spoke to me. I understood them. The more I read them the more my faith began to grow. I really believed that like the psalmist, God would hear my prayer and that he would help me. At that time the gospel began to come alive. I started to believe in Jesus. Each night I would lay facedown on my bedroom floor and cry out to him in simple prayers. I told God that I was hurting, and I asked him to help me. After some weeks I began to feel the presence of God as I prayed. The first time I sensed God's presence I was really surprised. After my initial astonishment I began to feel a deep joy in my heart. My heart was still broken and I felt pain and sadness, but amazingly I also had joy. I never before thought it was possible to feel pain and experience joy at the same time.

"The experience of joy gave me hope. I asked God to take away my pain, but all I felt the Lord say to me was, 'do not be afraid. I will not abandon you.' He was telling me that he wouldn't take away my pain but that he would be with me in the midst of the pain. I didn't like the answer. I wanted the pain to go away.

"I was angry with my wife for betraying me, and I was complaining to God about her. In the midst of my complaining I heard God tell me to repent of my own sins. This was the most important thing the Holy Spirit taught me. I was convinced that she was the bad guy and I was the good guy. I began to see my own limitations as a husband and father. I could see how I had sacrificed everything for my career. This was the point of real conversion for me. I knew I needed to repent.

"Around this time I was attending a workshop in a neighboring state where I met some people who were active in the Catholic charismatic renewal. They told me about the baptism in the Holy Spirit and offered to pray with me. I received the gift of tongues and my heart was filled with even more joy. When I returned home I attended a prayer meeting in my parish. There I met brothers and sisters who encouraged me and helped minister God's healing power to my life. I gradually began to feel a genuine interior restoration.

"As time passed I began to be less preoccupied with my own needs and felt a real desire to reach out to others. I began to notice how many people around me, at work, in our parish, were hurting and in need of encouragement in the Lord. I spoke to many of them, and I felt a desire to pray with them, but I was afraid to initiate. I told friends in the prayer group I'd been feeling a desire to pray with people but I didn't know how or if I should. They offered to pray with me for a greater freedom to follow the leading of the Lord. I sat in a chair, with my eyes closed, with my hands open in a posture of receptivity. As they prayed, I began to feel a burning sensation in my hands. I peeked open my eyes to see if anyone had lit a match or something, but no one had.

I told my friends my hands felt like they were burning and they told me that they believed the Lord was simply encouraging me to be willing to pray for healing with people when the opportunity arose.

"During this period of time my whole orientation to work changed. I felt a deep commitment to professional excellence, but I was no longer driven by fear or career ambition. I began to work more closely with my graduate students to encourage their personal development— the spiritual, emotional, physical, and relational dimensions of their life, as well as their scientific development. I encouraged my students to become excellent scientists with balanced wholesome lives.

"For the past twelve years I have led a weekly noon hour Bible study in Agronomy Hall at Iowa State. I've had many opportunities to speak with students and colleagues about Jesus Christ. In 1989, one of my Chinese graduate students shared with me the fear and the sadness he felt as he watched the violence unfold during the Tiannamin Square incident in Beijing. He admitted that he was deeply afraid for his family and friends back in China. I told him that I was a Christian and I offered to pray for him and his family. He said he had no religious background and that he did not know how to pray. I invited him to my office where we talked and I prayed. A couple of days later I took him to a meeting where a man gave his Christian testimony. The talk touched this student's heart and he asked to know more about Jesus. We spoke at length and the more we spoke the more interested he became. I shared the basic gospel message with him and we prayed together. He invited Jesus to come into his heart.

"Our prayer that day was simple, yet the Lord heard his prayer. The young man cried openly as we prayed and he told me, 'I felt the love of God come into my heart.' We started to meet on a weekly basis to read the bible, pray, and answer questions. He grew in faith and decided to join the Chinese faith community near the university.

"Over the past decade a number of Chinese students have come to the Bible study. They know little or nothing about God. They come initially saying they do not believe there is a God, yet they are always carrying burdens for which they are happy to receive prayer. Another one of my students told me that he had received a transfusion of tainted blood and was now having liver problems. Doctors told him he needed a biopsy to determine the proper amount of medication he would need for his liver condition. He was afraid. I asked if he would like me to pray for healing. He said yes. A couple of my friends and I prayed with him just before he left for his liver biopsy. I accompanied him to the hospital for his biopsy.

"A few days later he received a call from the doctor saying he would not need the medication because his liver was in fine condition. He was deeply impacted by this series of events. Our relationship deepened and we began to speak about Jesus together. He graduated and returned to China. Our friendship in Christ remains to this day."

Empowered for Mission

Bob's story provides a vivid example of the transforming effects of the Spirit's work in our day. His encounter with the Lord Jesus in the Holy Spirit produced real change in him. Bob was changed from an ambitious, career-centered man, indifferent to God's call in his life, into a friend of God and a living witness to the mercy and power of Jesus Christ.

The road Bob traveled was from brokenness and despair, to the experience of the joy of the Lord; from encounter with God to repentance, which in turn led him to fellowship with others. Fellowship provided the context for healing and restoration which opened him up, and set him free from self-preoccupation, allowing him to be aware of the needs of others. The process ultimately led to mission, to an empowerment that moved him to pass on to others the grace he himself had received.

Bob knew without doubt that the Lord had rescued him. Like the psalmist he could say:

"I love the Lord, because he has heard my voice and my supplications. Because he inclined his ear to me, therefore I will call on him as long as I live.... Gracious is the Lord and righteous; our God is merciful. The Lord preserves the simple; when I was brought low, he saved me" (Ps 116:1-2, 5-6).

The grace of the Holy Spirit led Bob to become a witness. He was moved and inspired to pass on the reality he himself had received. He knew who the Lord was and what he could do.

Bob is an example of what Pope John Paul II means when he says, "the marvels of Pentecost have not ceased, but are renewed abundantly in the Church today."[1] This is the "New Pentecost." The move of the Spirit in our day is meant to lead to an awakening of faith, to changed lives, and to a passion to make Jesus Christ known to the whole world. As in every age of the Church, the Spirit is bestowing power for mission. The life-changing encounter with the risen Christ in the power of the Holy Spirit is the irreplaceable starting point. Authentic mission arises from this encounter.

Consider the first Pentecost. What happened that day? The apostles were waiting in the upper room as Jesus had commanded. He told them to "wait for the promise of Father." He said they would be "baptized with the Holy Spirit" and through that experience they would "receive power," enabling them to become Jesus' "witnesses ... to the end of the earth" (Acts 1:4-5, 8). The "promise" of the Father is the Holy Spirit.

They waited in the upper room. St. Luke gives his account of what took place that day:

"When the day of Pentecost had come, they were all together in one place. And suddenly a sound came from heaven like the rush of a mighty wind, and it filled all the house where they were sitting. And there appeared to them tongues as of fire, distributed and resting on each one of them. And they were all filled with the Holy Spirit and began to speak in other tongues, as the Spirit gave them utterance" (Acts 2:1-4).

The coming of the Spirit thrust the apostles out of the Upper Room and into the streets of Jerusalem. The experience of the Spirit changed them: "The gift of the Spirit had released their deepest energies, concentrating them on the mission entrusted to them by Jesus."[2] The mission entrusted to them was the public witness to the reality of the passion, death, resurrection, and ascension of Jesus Christ. The entire second chapter of the Acts of the Apostles is a proclamation by St. Peter, of the fact of Jesus' death and resurrection and his reigning in power. The coming of the Spirit is the fruit of Christ's having been "exalted at the right hand of God." Christ received the "promised Holy Spirit" from the Father and he in turn poured out that same Holy Spirit on the apostles.

The Spirit moved them to bear witness. He empowered their proclamation. He confirmed the message within them, giving them an unshakeable conviction and a profound clarity about God's plan revealed in Christ Jesus. St. Peter's message culminates in this exchange:

"'Let all the house of Israel therefore know assuredly that God has made him Lord and Christ, this Jesus whom you crucified.' Now when they had heard this they were cut to the heart, and said to Peter and the rest of the apostles, 'Brethren, what shall we do?' And Peter said to them, 'Repent, and be baptized every one of you in the name of Jesus Christ for the forgiveness of your sins; and you shall receive the gift of the Holy Spirit. For the promise is to you and to your children and to all that are far off, every one whom the Lord our God calls to him.... Save yourselves from this crooked generation'" (Acts 2:36-39, 40).

The central message of the apostles on Pentecost was simply this: "God has made him Lord and Christ, this Jesus whom you crucified." Pentecost was the Spirit-inspired proclamation, by tongue-speaking Galilean Jews, to "devout men from every nation under heaven," that Jesus Christ is Lord of all! Because he is Lord, all that he said has been vindicated. Now nothing can take precedence over the call to repentance. It's a matter of life and death.

The purpose of the Holy Spirit's coming is to make it possible for human beings to see and respond to what God has accomplished in his Son Jesus Christ. The Spirit bestows the "riches of assured understanding and the knowledge of God's mystery, of Christ, in whom are hid all the treasures of wisdom and knowledge" (Col 2:2-3). The Spirit reveals the mystery of Christ to the human spirit. That revelation comes in power; when it is received and obeyed it leads to a transformed life.

The Spirit comes to catch us up into what theologians have called the "Trinitarian missions." Christianity is the religion that begins in the heart of God. God goes in search of man who is lost. The Father sends his Son, who becomes one of us. He is God with us, revealing the truth about God's love and purpose for the human race. He demonstrates the infinite depth of that love through his death on the cross, and by means of that death makes it possible for human beings to enter the Father's house. Through his resurrection and ascension he returns to the Father and takes his seat upon the throne of glory where he will reign forever as Lord of all.

Christ's return to the glory of the Father makes it possible for the Spirit to be poured out on the earth. The Spirit comes as one who is sent by the Father and the Son to bestow on men and women the life Christ has won for them. The Church is born of the Spirit's coming. The Church is not just another historical religious organization, created by men to do good things in the world. The Church is born of the Holy Spirit. It is a divine creation. What makes the Church the Church is the indwelling presence and power of the Holy Spirit.

Born of the Holy Spirit the Church shares the Spirit's missionary purpose. Mission, that is, making known the mystery of Christ, is the reason she exists: "Evangelizing is in fact the grace and vocation proper to the Church, her deepest identity. She exists in order to evangelize."[3] The Church's reason for being is to bring to every person "the unsearchable riches of Christ" (Eph 3:8). This is the "gospel of God," (1 Thes 2:2); it is the "good news" within which is found "the power of God for salvation to everyone who has faith" (Rom 1:16).

God has fully revealed himself in his Son Jesus Christ for the salvation of the whole world. The Spirit comes to make that salvation a reality in the hearts and minds of men and women. The Church, when she is awake to the Spirit's presence and impulse, is always being led to proclaim Christ. It is her nature to do so: "the definitive self-revelation of God is the fundamental reason why the Church is missionary by her very nature. She cannot do other than proclaim the Gospel."[4]

By means of the Holy Spirit the gospel "takes shape in human minds and hearts and extends through history."[5] This gospel comes "not only in word, but also in power and in the Holy Spirit and with full conviction" (1 Thes 1:5). God's truth, the marvelous truth about Jesus Christ, is communicated to the human heart through the power of the Holy Spirit who imparts "full conviction" about who Jesus is.

This is the meaning of Pentecost. The "New Pentecost" is a return to these fundamental realities of the faith. The Spirit's movement in our time is meant to lead to a living experience of these realities. Bob's story gives us a glimpse of what the Spirit is saying to all of us. His story has been, and continues to be, repeated in the lives of millions of people throughout the world in our day.

Bob can say like St. Paul that the gospel came to him, "in power and in the Holy Spirit and with full conviction." He knows it's true because it changed him. He didn't simply receive historical information about Jesus to meditate upon, he met Jesus himself, the living, reigning Christ. And that encounter, which was made possible by the grace of the Holy Spirit, completely changed him. That experiential knowledge of Christ led Bob from the pit of despair into a life filled with genuine joy and hope. He was led from darkness to light, from a condition of slavery to freedom.

The Spirit came not only to help Bob deal with his personal problems, he came to get Bob to move out of the constricted circle of his own self-concern and to take up the mission God had made him for. Bob was set free not only from something, but he was freed for something. He was released from bondage to fear, bitterness, and shame, so that he could live in love.

St. Paul said, "we have the same spirit of faith as he had who wrote, 'I believed, and so I spoke,' we too believe, and so we speak.... For the love of Christ controls us, because we are convinced that one has died for all; therefore, all have died. And he died for all, that those who live might live no longer for themselves but for him who for their sake died and was raised" (2 Cor 4:13; 5:14-15).

Bob believed and so he spoke—to friends, to family, to colleagues, to students about what Christ had done for him. By the present action of the Spirit, the love of Christ has begun to control Bob. The Spirit is reproducing in Bob the very reality which St. Paul himself experienced. He was moved to live no longer for himself but for Christ. Life is no longer defined by personal ambition. With St. Paul he can say, "it is no longer I who live, but Christ who lives in me; and the life I now live in the flesh I live by faith in the Son of God, who loved me and gave himself for me" (Gal 2:20).

A life surrendered to the movement of the Holy Spirit necessarily leads to evangelization and mission. The Spirit has come to complete the saving work of Jesus Christ on the earth, to awaken our race, and to bring us back to God. To do that he transforms us into "ambassadors for Christ," so that the Spirit himself can, "[make] his appeal through us"(2 Cor 5:20). This is how God intends to bring salvation to the world.

God wants to reach out to the world through those whom he has touched and transformed. Out of humility and genuine compassion Bob was moved to share the truth about what Christ had done for him. Evangelization has nothing to do with imposing oneself upon another. It is a humble appeal from one broken sinner to another, to come home to God: "we beseech you on behalf of Christ, be reconciled to God. For our sake he made him to be sin who knew no sin, so that in him we might become the righteousness of God" (2 Cor 5:20-21).

The Spirit transformed Bob into a witness. He remains a world-class agronomist, committed to excellence as a teacher, but now he is also guided by the missionary impulse the Holy Spirit has awakened within him. Over the past ten years Bob's story has touched the lives of dozens of colleagues throughout the world. Bob's work has taken him to a number of countries in the former Soviet Union, Africa, and China. Because he is alert and docile to the promptings of the Spirit he has not only been able to help his colleagues on a professional level, but he has led many of them into a relationship with Christ.

A Time of Mobilization

The Holy Spirit is bringing about a "New Pentecost" in the Church today because we are in desperate need of it. Many, including the Holy Father, recognize that the Church in many places has lost its missionary zeal. Religious orders that were once burning with a passion to bring the message of the gospel to the world no longer see the need to evangelize. They assume all men and women are already saved, so their work is reduced to this world's goals. Their horizon has been flattened and dulled. Because of their lack of vision and purpose many of those orders are gradually disappearing. They have lost their message. They have nothing to say that any social service organization couldn't say just as well.

But the Church is not primarily a social service organization. She is a reality born of the Spirit and sent to free men and women from ultimate human despair. She is the sign of eternal hope for the world. She bears the message that comes from the Father's house. She opens up the possibility of eternity, of heaven, of everlasting joy for every human being.

When the Church loses sight of this mission, when she yields to the spirit of the age, she loses her power and dynamism. She has nothing to say to the world. The bride of Christ begins to look old, feeble, out of touch, and irrelevant. She seems powerless in the face of the juggernaut of worldliness that surrounds her. She loses her dynamism because she has stopped listening to the Holy Spirit. When she insists on preaching a message other than the gospel in all its purity and clarity, when she seeks to be something other than what she was meant to be, the Spirit of God will not support it. Hence, she is rendered powerless. The Holy Spirit has been sent to empower the Church to proclaim the gospel. When it is declared and lived wholeheartedly the Church has power. She is sharp, clear, alive, effective, dynamic, compelling, challenging, radical, and attractive. When she compromises she steps out from under the anointing of the Spirit and she is left to her own resources, which in the face of the forces set against her, leaves her ineffective, weak, and singularly unattractive.

God has promised that the gates of hell will never prevail against the Church. That is a rock solid guarantee. But it does not mean that even large portions of the Church will not fall into compromise with the spirit of the age. It is simply a fact of history: "It can happen," says Cardinal Ratzinger "that the Church makes herself impenetrable to the Spirit of God which gives her life."[6] Religious leaders today can fall prey to the same temptation St. Stephen accused the High Priest and the elders of Israel of: "You stiff-necked people, uncircumcised in heart and ears, you always resist the Holy Spirit. As your fathers did, so do you" (Acts 7:51).

The temptation of Church leaders is to replace the dynamism of the Spirit with more institution or more organization. Yet as Ratzinger points out, "it is not correct to pretend that everything must plug into a uniform organization; better to have less organization and more Holy Spirit."[7] An overemphasis and dependence on institution ultimately renders the church incapable of fulfilling her mission. As Cardinal Ratzinger explains:

> There are real reasons for fearing that the Church might take on too many institutions of human law that then become like Saul's armor which prevented young David from walking. It is always necessary to study whether institutions that were useful in the past are still useful today. The only institutional element the Church needs is the one the Lord gave her; the sacramental structure of the people of God, centered on the Eucharist ... the only ministry indispensable in the Church is the priesthood.[8]

Young David did not need the armor of King Saul to destroy the giant Goliath who was set against the army of Israel. All he needed was what God had given him to face what looked like impossible odds. Saul's offer of his armor to David was sensible given the power of his foe. Yet David's strength was not to be found in the armor of the King, but in the Spirit of the Lord. To rely on Saul's armor rather than on what God had given David rendered him powerless and immobile.

We are living at a moment in the history of the Church when she is rediscovering that the "institutional and charismatic aspects are co-essential to the Church's constitution."[9] The Spirit is bringing a corrective to the Church. There has been an overemphasis upon the institutional dimension of the Church. The Church cannot capture the minds and hearts of unbelievers, or even her own children for that matter, by relying simply upon organizational and institutional structures.

The rediscovery of the charismatic dimension essentially means being attentive to the present action of the Holy Spirit and being receptive to all of its gifts. The Church is not a museum that preserves important artifacts. She is a living organism, vivified by the power and presence of the Spirit. She is a dynamic reality, moving throughout history with one purpose and goal: to proclaim Christ Jesus.

The whole biblical understanding of the Spirit is one of movement and dynamism:

"The fundamental idea expressed in the biblical name of the Spirit is, therefore, not an intellectual power, but that of a dynamic impulse, similar to the force of wind. In the Bible, the primary function of the Spirit is not to give understanding, but to give movement; not to shed light but to impart dynamism."[10]

A few years ago I had the privilege of collaborating on a series of evangelistic events with a dynamic young Hungarian lay leader named Zoltan. He is a very bright, talented young Catholic intellectual who has played a key role in some dynamic evangelistic work going on in Hungary. Struck by his passion for souls and the clarity with which he preached the gospel, I asked him where the zeal and energy came from.

He told me that he had been a Catholic for many years, but there was a time when the Lord gave him a passion and fire to proclaim the gospel. He said he was attending a seminar on the meaning of the kerygma, that is, the basic core message of the gospel. During the talks the speaker broke down the fundamental elements of the gospel as it was preached in the Acts of the Apostles. Zoltan said that as the speaker was addressing them throughout the day he felt a fire burning within him, growing more intense as the day progressed. He said the words of the gospel filled his heart with joy and he experienced a new release of an interior dynamism and energy.

By the time the last talk was completed, he was so filled with energy he went outside the conference center where they were meeting and he ran around the building ten times, laughing, singing, and giving praise to God. He was so happy he felt like his heart was going to burst. That experience produced a permanent change in him. He was simply given a gift from the Lord, a new desire to read Scripture and a passion to proclaim the gospel. The Holy Spirit opened his mind to the beauty and majesty of Christ and that knowledge set his heart on fire.

Charisms

Zoltan received a gift from the Spirit, a charism. Charism means gift, a manifestation of the Holy Spirit. St. Paul says, "to each is given the manifestation of the Spirit for the common good" (1 Cor 12:7). The Church reminds us that the Holy Spirit "distributes special graces among the faithful of every rank. By these gifts he makes them fit and ready to undertake various tasks and offices for the renewal and building up of the Church."[11] Charisms impart to a person the power of God that will make them capable of doing the work of God.

The New Testament provides various lists of these gifts[12] which include healing, prophecy, tongues, interpretation of tongues, discernment, administration, the gift of helps, teaching, preaching and so on. The gifts are varied but all are directed toward building up the body in love. My purpose here isn't to give a full presentation of the gifts, but to simply point out that the rediscovery of the charismatic dimension of the Church has led to the reemergence of the charisms of the Holy

Spirit. Openness to the movement of the Spirit allows the gifts the Lord has given to equip his people to surface.

For many Catholics these gifts "are often repressed and buried."[13] In fact it is not an exaggeration to say that for many Catholics the gifts of the Spirit given at baptism and confirmation remain hidden their entire lives. That lack of responsiveness to the presence and power of the Holy Spirit deadens the Church's apostolic zeal and leaves her incapable of meeting the challenges of contemporary culture.

On the other hand, when the gifts of the Spirit are welcomed, and are exercised with discernment and guided by charity, things happen: "Some charisms given by the Spirit burst in like an impetuous wind, which seizes people and carries them to new ways of missionary commitment to the radical service of the gospel."[14] That is exactly what the Holy Spirit wants to produce in every disciple: a new missionary commitment to the radical service of the gospel. The Spirit wants to make us all radical. He's coming in our day to burn away the spiritual sloth and the lukewarmness that has poisoned so much of the Church in the West in this century. The Spirit of God, who is pure fire and love, cannot dwell in a heart, or in a Church, that is lukewarm. Jesus made it perfectly clear how he responds to lukewarmness: "I know your works: you are neither cold nor hot. Would that you were cold or hot! So, because you are lukewarm, and neither cold nor hot, I will spew you out of my mouth" (Rv 3:15-16).

To be tepid in the face of Christ's offer of salvation, of his command to "go make disciples of all nations," and to the offer of the spiritual gifts he has won for us through his death, resurrection, and ascension, is a profound affront to God. The only response appropriate to the initiative of the Spirit in our lives is all-out surrender and a burning zeal for the mission Christ has called us to.

St. Bonaventure's description of St. Francis provides a glimpse of where the Holy Spirit wants to lead us:

> Like a sharp sword all on fire, zeal for the salvation of others
> pierced the depths of his heart ... this was the reason why he was
> so energetic in prayer, so active in preaching; this is why he went
> beyond all limits to give a good example ... for the sake of good
> example he inflicted frequent penances and burdens on himself
> ... no one seems to worry nowadays about the harm which the
> Devil is doing, but Francis used to shed tears every day for his
> own sins and the sins of others.[15]

We aren't there yet, and maybe in this life we will never reach the
heights Francis touched, but we must see that the Spirit has more for
us. He wants to produce a zeal for the salvation of others, a desire for
prayer and a genuine sorrow for our sins and the sins of the world.
When the Spirit revives a soul that is what he produces: a passion for
holiness and mission. The call to radical discipleship may seem far off
and unreachable, but if we look closely we can see that the Spirit is
already moving on a wide scale to lead the Church in that direction.

The Hour of the Laity

The reemergence of the charisms has led to a flowering of an apostolic
impulse within the laity:

"It is possible to speak of a new lay life, rich in immense human
potential, as an historically observable and verifiable fact. The true
value of this life comes from the Holy Spirit, who abundantly bestows
his gifts on the Church, as he has done since the beginning on the day
of Pentecost (cf. Acts 2:3-4; 1 Cor 12:7-11). In our day too, many
signs and great witness have been given by individuals, groups and
movements generously dedicated to the apostolate. They show that the
marvels of Pentecost have not ceased, but are renewed abundantly in
the Church today. It is obvious that in addition to a considerable

development in the doctrine of charisms, there has also been a new flowering of active lay people in the Church: it is not by chance that the two facts have occurred at the same time. All this is the work of the Holy Spirit...."[16]

The new emerging laity, enflamed with apostolic zeal, is the direct result of the outpouring of charisms. The Spirit is awakening a sleeping giant. This stirring is expressed concretely as individuals, empowered by the Spirit, come together for the sake of mission. Our time has seen the flourishing of new lay movements such as Focolare, Communion in Liberation, and the charismatic renewal; dynamic new religious orders, seminaries, houses of formation, retreat centers, and houses of religious sisters have begun. A wide range of ministries has emerged as well, including ministries to the poor, the elderly, and the unborn; new television networks, a steadily growing number of radio stations, magazines, newspapers, and a dynamic, effective apologetics movement are all signs of the present action of the Holy Spirit.

I believe this is only the beginning. The "dawning of a new missionary age"[17] is upon us. From the highest levels of leadership within the Catholic Church a call is coming forward for a fresh "proclamation of the Word that saves, and the audacious witness of faith in a renewed missionary endeavor."[18]

That Holy Spirit is calling for an "audacious witness of faith." Webster's New Collegiate Dictionary defines "audacious" as being, "intrepidly daring, adventurous, bold, and marked by originality and verve." The Holy Spirit wants to give us new boldness, creativity, and courage, to reclaim the great adventure of Christian discipleship. The lukewarm, timid, politicized, secularized version of Christianity, which has gripped the Church in our time, has had its day. A new day has dawned, a day born of the Spirit in power.

One Man's Response

Vernon is a meat cutter working at Safeway Foods in Vancouver, British Columbia. Born in Scotland, he is a lifelong Catholic whose faith was awakened nearly thirty years ago through the experience of the baptism in the Holy Spirit. The baptism in the Spirit awakened within him a desire to read the Scriptures and to share his faith.

He began reading Scripture daily and as he did he encountered the person of Christ in a deep way. The word of God became manna for him. As he devoured God's word, a passion to preach the gospel and share his faith began to grow within him.

He shared his faith whenever he could, with friends, colleagues, and even strangers when he felt led. He began a small prayer group and developed simple teachings on how to pray for the conversion and the spiritual development of one's children.

Over time the yearning to preach intensified, but being a lay Catholic he wasn't quite sure where or how to express that desire. His priest friends encouraged him to follow the Spirit's lead.

Vernon decided to establish a School of Evangelization, a place where Catholics could receive systematic training in evangelization, where they could receive a clear presentation of the gospel and be trained to share the gospel with others.

The school was thirteen weeks long, one night per week, and it ended with four weeks of visitations. Those who were trained were given names from local parishes of inactive Catholics. The students went door to door to share their faith and invite people to recommit their lives to the Lord Jesus.

The school was a great success and it led to ten more schools over the next five years. Over eight hundred people went through the training. With the help of some of his graduates and in collaboration with the office of evangelization in the archdiocese of Vancouver, Vernon began to organize large, dynamic conferences on evangelization, mission and the work of the Holy Spirit.

From there he spearheaded the development of Catholic Alpha Courses for parishes in the Vancouver Archdiocese. More than twenty parishes are currently using the course as a means of evangelization and hundreds of people have been brought to Christ and into the fuller life in the Holy Spirit.

I've had the privilege of working with Vernon. He is a very gifted, anointed preacher and teacher. His passion for the Word of God and for the mission of Christ is contagious. I once listened to him address a gathering of some eighty-five priests on the call of the Holy Spirit in our day. He spoke with power, conviction, and authority. Some of the priests were visibly moved by his words and surprised by the wisdom he had.

I could almost hear their thoughts as they listened attentively to Vernon: "Isn't this man a meat cutter? How does he know all this? Where does he get such authority?" I was deeply touched that day as I watched Vernon, a man with the equivalence of a high school education, address a room filled with religious professionals, educated men, scholars, and bishops. He was helping them see what the Spirit was saying to the Church.

I thought of the words of St. Paul, "And I was with you in weakness and in much fear and trembling; and my speech and my message were not in plausible words of wisdom, but in the demonstration of the Spirit and power, that your faith might not rest on the wisdom of men, but the power of God" (1 Cor 2:3-5).

Vernon had something to say that day because he embraced all that the Spirit had for him nearly thirty years earlier.

EIGHT

An Eternal Perspective

For this slight momentary affliction is preparing for us an eternal weight of glory beyond all comparison, because we look not to the things that are seen but to the things that are unseen.

2 CORINTHIANS 4:17-18

Three years ago I was asked to give a series of talks on the core elements of the gospel to a small group of Carmelite Sisters in Kazakhstan. The sisters lived in a small convent that they reclaimed after the fall of communism. It was in considerable disrepair and was in the process of being remodeled during my visit.

The sisters, about ten of them, were a joyful, hardworking, and faith-filled group. Before the retreat began I met most of the sisters, including the Mother Superior. She was in her early sixties and had been a nun for more than forty years. She reminded me of Mother Teresa of Calcutta—she was small, slightly hunched, energetic, and carried a great deal of spiritual authority. She radiated holiness.

As we began the first day, I looked out at the sisters, and wondered why I was speaking to them. I was convinced that I had more to learn from them than they did from me. Feeling a bit humbled by their genuine holiness and passion for Christ, I pressed on with the talks.

The first day went well. The second day we were just about to begin, when the Mother Superior got up from her seat and left the room. I asked through my translator where she went and no one seemed to know. I decided to wait until she returned before getting started.

After a few moments the door opened and she came in with about fifteen men and women who had been working on the remodeling project for the convent. They were a rough-looking crowd. Dressed in old work clothes, covered with sawdust and white powder from the concrete mixture, they obediently followed the Mother Superior's directions to sit down. From where I was standing, they didn't look very happy.

The Mother Superior came up to me, and through my translator said, "Preach to them. Tell them about Jesus." She told me they were Christians, Muslims, and unbelievers, and that some of them might have been baptized at one time in their lives, but that most of them, even if they were baptized, no longer practiced their faith.

She looked at me with determination and said, "Go ahead, teach them." She sat down in the first row and I turned to the group. They were clearly uncomfortable and didn't want to be there. I gave a few brief introductory comments, and tried to break the ice a bit with a humorous story, but it flopped. The workers just sat and stared at me while the sisters smiled politely at everything I said.

That morning I gave two talks, focusing on the love of God poured out for us in the passion, death, and resurrection of Jesus. By the end of the first talk I could tell most of the men and women were beginning to feel more comfortable and were quite receptive to what I was saying. But there was one man sitting in the last row who stared at me with an intense, angry look on his face the entire time I spoke. He was an intimidating-looking man; he was very large, with broad shoulders, a thick neck, square jaw, and deep-set eyes.

At the end of the talks I invited anyone who wanted to make a response to the message or who would like prayer to come forward. A number of them immediately came forward to receive prayer from our team. After nearly a half hour the man in the back row came forward. He came right up to me, but didn't say anything. I turned to the translator and asked what I could do for this man. He said, "I need help."

He had done something wrong and wanted to know if God could forgive him.

I asked him what he had done, but he bowed his head in silence. After a few minutes I asked him again, and he responded, "I killed my brother." The man went on to tell his story. Eight years earlier, his brother had come home to their mother's house drunk. His brother was loud and violent, yelling at their mother. The man tried to subdue his brother and a fight ensued. This man lost control of himself and killed his brother with his own hands.

He spent five years in jail for his crime. While he was in jail, his mother died and he was unable to go to her in her time of need. There were no other family members to take care of her. He felt an enormous burden of guilt for what he had done, and felt that God was punishing him by not allowing him to help his mother. He said he knew he deserved to be punished but wondered if God could forgive him.

We spoke for a few moments about the love and mercy of God and I asked him if he would like us to pray with him. He nodded. I placed my hand on his shoulder and began to pray, asking the Holy Spirit to hear his cry and to free him from the weight of sin, guilt, and anger that was pressing in on him. After the brief prayer we stood quietly, each with our eyes closed. After a few moments he began to weep; the love of Christ was pouring over him and all he could do was cry. We prayed with him for some time and at the end of the day, this rock-hard and angry man could do nothing but smile.

The next day we came back for the final session of the retreat. The Mother Superior told me that she had spent most of the previous evening talking to the man with whom I had prayed. She said he was like a starving child, hungry for spiritual food and that the Lord had touched him deeply. He had no other family, and after speaking together for some time, both of them felt the Lord was calling him to serve the sisters as a custodian. They would provide a place for him to receive the spiritual food that he needed and he in turn would look after the physical needs of the convent.

In an act of gratitude for the forgiveness he had received he wanted to offer something back to God and thus prepare himself for heaven. The touch of the Holy Spirit released him from bondage and hopelessness, and gave him a glimpse of the depths of Jesus' love and power. For eight years a black cloud hung over this man's head, but in a moment's time, it was dispelled by the power of the Holy Spirit. In its place was born the hope of heaven. This man knew that Jesus died to free him from the grave sin he committed against his own mother's son. No doubt the road ahead for him will require purification and continued healing. But what is certain is that he knows by the gentle touch of the Spirit, that Jesus left the ninety-nine sheep to go in search of him, the one who was lost, in order that he might be found and brought home to the Father's house. He is on his way home.

Restoring an Eternal Perspective

The experience of the Holy Spirit helps to restore an eternal perspective. The man in the story above caught a glimpse of eternity. By the grace of the Spirit, heaven was opened to him in a new way. This is one of the most important aspects of what the Spirit is doing in our day. He is giving a taste of heaven in order to bring hope to birth in a world that increasingly works to seal itself off from the voice of God.

The denial of God and the consequent secularization of our culture has made it very difficult to maintain an authentic biblical worldview. Man's horizon is limited to the here and now. Through the personal experience of the Spirit, heaven breaks through that limited horizon. The Spirit helps us to see Christ risen, the Lord of heaven and earth, who is "the living one" and who is "alive forever more" (Rv 1:18).

By the grace of the Spirit we begin to touch eternity. We are made capable of seeing "what no eye has seen, nor ear has heard" (1 Cor 2:9).

As St. Paul says we have "tasted the heavenly gift, and have become partakers of the Holy Spirit, and have tasted the goodness of the word of God and the powers of the age to come" (Heb 6:4-5). The Spirit releases within us the "powers of the age to come." That experience helps to awaken the theological virtue of hope.

Hope has been defined as "the confident expectation of fulfillment." By the gift of the Holy Spirit, we are capable of seeing our own future, that is, the possibility of heaven, revealed in the resurrected, reigning life of Jesus of Nazareth. The Spirit produces within us a genuine confidence that our lives will find their fulfillment in eternity with Christ Jesus.

The Spirit gives us the power to know who we are and where our lives are headed. The Spirit breaks the power of the isolation and fear that a life without hope of eternity necessarily produces in the human heart. It bears "witness with our Spirit that we are children of God, and if children, then heirs, heirs of God and fellow heirs with Christ" (Rom 8:16-17).

Reorienting Our Vision

The Spirit wants to change our scales of measurement by giving us a glimpse of eternity. The taste of heaven opens up our horizon and sets us free from a disordered attachment to the things of this world and enables us to put our life here on earth in proper perspective. By the grace of the Spirit we don't have to pretend that life here on earth is something more than it is. We don't have to create a make believe world in order to distract ourselves from the hard realities of life. We can face the difficult fact that "the form of this world is passing away" (1 Cor 7:31), and our own life "is like an evening shadow" that will "wither away like grass" (Ps 102:11).

It is only by the grace of the Spirit that we can say like St. Paul,

"So we do not lose heart. Though our outer nature is wasting away, our inner nature is being renewed every day. For this slight momentary affliction is preparing for us an eternal weight of glory beyond all comparison, because we look not to the things that are seen but to the things that are unseen; for the things that are seen are transient, but the things that are unseen are eternal" (2 Cor 4:16-18).

The Spirit strengthens our heart and renews our inner nature by enabling us to actually see by faith the "eternal weight of glory" that is set before us. The Spirit makes us capable of seeing and living our lives according to what is unseen. The glory set before us is not "pie in the sky" wishful thinking or escapism for those who lack the courage to admit this life is all there is. We know better. We are given a genuine conviction, a life-changing revelation, and a true knowledge of the things to come. This wisdom cannot be taken away, because it comes directly from the Spirit: "And we all, with unveiled face, beholding the glory of the Lord, are being changed into his likeness from one degree of glory to the another; for this comes from the Lord who is the Spirit" (2 Cor 3:18).

The glory that we see, which we know by the assurance of the Holy Spirit, is given to us in Jesus. It's in seeing him that we see our destiny: "But our commonwealth is in heaven, and from it we await a Savior, the Lord Jesus Christ, who will change our lowly body to be like his glorious body, by the power which enables him even to subject all things to himself" (Phil 3:20-21).

Understanding Time

The hope of heaven gives the human heart the freedom to grasp distinctly the meaning of our time here on earth. Jesus made it clear that our life here is a trial; the decisions we make on a daily basis have eternal significance.

He has told us in his word that, "the end of all things is at hand" (1 Pt 4:7), and that we are living in the "last hour" (1 Jn 2:18). The Lord himself has taught us that, "the present time is the time of Spirit and witness, but also a time marked by 'distress' and the trial of evil which does not spare the Church and ushers in the struggles of the last days. It is a time of waiting and watching."[1]

The Church lives between the two comings of Christ. He came first as a lamb, to be sacrificed for us, and thereby making it possible for us to enter the Kingdom of God. But he will "come again in glory to judge the living and the dead."[2] We are all destined to face judgment. Upon his return in glory, he "will bring to light the things now hidden in darkness and will disclose the purposes of the heart" (1 Cor 4:5). "Then will the culpable unbelief that counted the offer of God's grace as nothing be condemned."[3]

The Spirit not only wants to bring conviction about the fact of Christ's coming in glory, he also comes to prepare us for that day. He wants to reveal to us now the true condition of our heart, and to show us the darkness that resides there—the hidden purposes that stand against God and his total claim on us. The Spirit wants all that is hidden to be revealed now, so it can be dealt with, subdued, and put to death before the day when our hearts will be manifested as they truly are before the eyes of him from whom nothing can be hidden: "And before him no creature is hidden, but all are open and laid bare to the eyes of him with whom we have to do" (Heb 4:13).

The Spirit gives us the courage to face our own impending death and "confidence for the day of judgment" (1 Jn 4:17). He brings that fear under control, replacing it with "a spirit of power and love and self-control" (2 Tm 1:7). We are made capable of letting go, of offering our life as a gift for others. We know we have been given "power to become children of God" (Jn 1:12), so we stand secure, guided by a living hope, placing our future in the hands of a loving Father.

As a child of God, having tasted of the good things to come, I know with confidence that despite what the world tells me, "man's life does not consist in the abundance of his possessions" (Lk 12:15). The Spirit wants to open the heavenly treasures to every human heart so we can understand what is truly valuable and enduring. All our possessions, money, and earthly treasures will pass away; only "the word of the Lord abides forever" (1 Pt 1:25). By the power of the Spirit we can face the temptations and lies of the devil that play upon our fears and insecurities and dupe us into believing we will find security in possessing and consuming things. Instead we can stand against the devil's schemes as Jesus did: "Man shall not live by bread alone, but by every word that proceeds from the mouth of God" (Mt 4:4).

In the freedom and security of the Spirit, we can learn to live in wisdom, becoming "rich toward God" (Lk 12:21). The Spirit has freed me to take Jesus' words literally:

"Do not lay up for yourselves treasures on earth, where moth and rust consume and where thieves break in and steal, but lay up for yourselves treasures in heaven, where neither moth nor rust consumes and where thieves do not break in and steal. For where your treasure is, there will your heart be also" (Mt 6:19-21).

Jesus asks us to be wise investors. If we take Jesus' words and invest in heaven, our hearts will follow. If our hearts are in heaven, we will live the life Jesus has called us to live here on earth.

If I know in the depths of my heart that God is my Father, and that he loves me infinitely, my present and future are secured: "I have learned, in whatever state I am, to be content. I know how to be abased, and I know how to abound" (Phil 4:11). I am set free to love others. This is what the Spirit wants to produce in us now. He wants to give us the freedom to love as Christ loved.

Remembering the Stakes

The Spirit wants to lead us to live a life that will prepare us to meet the Lord face-to-face. He wants us to see clearly the inescapable choice that is set before every one of us. C.S. Lewis gives a vivid description of what that day will bring:

> In the end that Face which is the delight or the terror of the universe must be turned upon each of us, either with one expression or with the other, either conferring glory inexpressible or inflicting shame that can never be cured or disguised ... we walk every day on the razor edge between these two incredible possibilities.[4]

No Fat Cats in the Kingdom of God

Dr. Dan Heffernan attended a retreat for men in 1982. He went on the retreat with a sincere desire to hear what the Lord wanted to say to him. The theme of the retreat focused on the lordship of Christ. The speakers challenged the men to honestly assess their lives in view of Christ's call to radical service of the Kingdom of God.

As Dan reflected on the talks he heard a very simple, clear word from the Lord: "You Dan, are a fat cat. There are no fat cats in my kingdom!" The word came to him with genuine conviction. He shared the word with the other men on the retreat. He left that weekend convinced the Lord wanted a change in his life.

Dan had always had a heart for the poor. Years earlier he helped found a free medical clinic near his home in mid-Michigan. But since he had relocated in a different town some years earlier, he no longer worked directly with the poor. The week following the retreat he asked the Lord each day to show him what he wanted him to do.

Within the next seven days, three different people came to him independently and suggested that Dan consider offering his time, talent, and resources to serve the needs of the poor and to minister to prisoners. He believed the Lord was speaking to him through these people. So in 1982 he began a free medical clinic near his home in Ypsilanti, Michigan.

He gathered volunteer workers and from a local school serving as a temporary clinic, he offered free medical care every Saturday during the year. The first year they saw, on average, fifteen patients per week. Since that time the clinic has relocated and is now serving nearly five thousand people per year. From that original vision, the clinic, which they eventually named Hope, has developed into a free dental clinic, a soup kitchen, a free laundry service called "Wash with Care," a halfway house, a restaurant called the "Oasis Café," a growing prison ministry that began in 1984, and free health education directed to help provide the poor with a sense of personal dignity and hope for their lives.

Dan responded to the prompting of the Spirit. The Spirit was leading Dan to move out of his comfort zone. The Lord wanted more from Dan, more of his time, his money, and his resources in order to build his kingdom. Dan said yes to the Spirit's prompting, and he made an investment in heaven, in the things the Lord wanted him to be concerned about. That investment has produced fruit in abundance, fruit that will flower into eternity.

Conclusion

Cooperating With the Spirit

The key to receiving all that the Lord has for each of us is to learn how to cooperate with the work of the Holy Spirit in our lives. Pope John Paul II has made the call to "docility to the Holy Spirit" a central theme of his entire pontificate. The abundant outpouring of the Spirit in this century is the heart of the Lord's provision for his Church in this difficult hour. The way ahead for all of us is found in a conscious, living relationship with the Holy Spirit.

What follows are seven keys to cooperating with the work of the Holy Spirit. This isn't intended to be an exhaustive list, but it does represent fundamental things we need to do in order to orient our hearts and minds to the movement of the Spirit:

1. Repent
The most important thing we can do to cooperate with the Spirit is to make a decisive break from our attachment to sin. That implies an honest assessment, or as our friends in Alcoholics Anonymous say, it requires a "searching moral inventory" of our lives. We need to decide to give up our pet sins. We need to allow the Holy Spirit to burn away the affection and attachment we have to the habit patterns of sin we've allowed to remain within us, and through which we still seek consolation, comfort and escape.

St. Paul tells us why: "To set the mind on the flesh is death, but to set the mind on the Spirit is life and peace" (Rom 8:6). The quickest way to kill the work of the Spirit in our lives is to feed our flesh. If we are looking to the flesh for consolation, we leave no room for the consolations of the Spirit. To receive all that the Spirit has for us demands an honest, decisive turning from sin and a turning toward the Lord and all he has for us.

2. Seek First the Kingdom

Jesus told his disciples, "Seek first his kingdom and his righteousness, and all these things shall be yours as well" (Mt 6:33). To seek the kingdom of God means to seek the King himself. Jesus makes it clear that he must be given the first place. Nothing can take precedence over his rule in our lives. The Spirit of God has come to open up to us the very life of God. The question before each of us is: do we want that life?

The only way to come into the life of the kingdom is to make it our first love, the thing we most want. If we put Jesus and his plan and purpose for our lives ahead of everything else, including career, family, relationships, money, entertainment, comfort, personal goals, etc., we will be able to walk in the fullness of the Spirit. The Spirit has come to lead us to the Father and to open up the very heart of God to us. If that is what we hunger and thirst for, we will experience the power of the Spirit. That is what the Spirit is interested in doing for us. He's come to give us heaven. If this is what we want, we will come to know the Spirit intimately. If not, he will remain a stranger, a mere doctrine rather than a person.

If we truly hunger for Jesus, the Spirit will lead us to those places he can be found. He will deepen our experience and hunger for the sacraments, he will open up the Scriptures, enliven the teaching of the Church, and he will reveal Jesus to us in our neighbor, and in particular, in the poor who are with us. He will empower us to see Jesus in all his disguises.

3. Earnestly Desire the Spiritual Gifts

St. Paul tells us to "earnestly desire the spiritual gifts" (1 Cor 14:1). This isn't a suggestion; it's a command. When Jesus took his seat upon the throne of heaven, he was given authority to pour out upon all flesh the gifts he had acquired through his death and resurrection. A central part of Jesus' plan of redemption is to endow his people with his gifts, powers that will enable us to share in his work of redemption. We cannot effectively do the work of the kingdom without the gifts and powers of the king: "Unless the Lord builds the house, those who build it labor in vain" (Ps 127:1). Hence, we are exhorted to earnestly desire the spiritual gifts. That means we need to make a conscious effort to understand what the gifts are, to actively discern what particular gifts we've been given, to pray for them, to welcome whatever gifts Jesus has for us, to use the gifts for the common good and to accept them with gratitude and humility, always keeping our hearts fixed not on the gift itself, but on the Giver of the gift.

4. Test Everything

Again, St. Paul tells us, "Do not quench the Spirit, do not despise prophesying, but test everything; hold fast to what is good" (1 Thess 5:19-21). Exercising spiritual gifts requires wisdom and discernment. Discerning the work of the Spirit can oftentimes be difficult, even frustrating. Spiritual gifts can easily be misused. They can be sought for their own sake, for the sake of experience or for a sense of power or prestige. They can and frequently are abused, because of sin and human weakness.

The difficulties that often accompany the exercise of the gifts can cause us to want to "quench the Spirit" or to simply ignore the importance and use of the gifts. St. Paul here is making it clear that ignoring the Spirit and his gifts is not an option. Once the source of a gift has been discerned, the gift should be received and exercised as love demands. Indeed, we are exhorted to "hold fast" to whatever is discerned as good.

5. Give God Permission

If you want a deeper relationship with the Holy Spirit, give God a blank check. Decide in your heart that you want whatever he wants for you, no matter what it is. Don't put limits on him. Be willing to come out of your comfort zones and the grooves you've dug to ensure your safety, comfort, and security. Tell the Lord every morning that your life is his and that you give him permission to do with it whatever he wants. Then walk throughout your day with one ear turned toward the Spirit. Don't leave the Spirit at home or in church. Be conscious of his presence; attempt to listen even amidst the noise and frantic pace of life. When you hear him, or sense his prompting or gentle nudge, act on it. Don't hesitate, do what he wants you to do. If you do this consistently, the Spirit will become your intimate friend and he will make something beautiful out of your life.

Pope John Paul II told the whole Church as we entered the third millennium, that the Spirit is leading us to, "put out into the deep." It's time for the Church to leave the shallow end of the pool; the purposes of Christ and the power of the Spirit are being released in the deep end. It's time for each one of us to dive into the deep water of the Spirit's purpose and will for us.

6. Run With the Saints

St. Paul describes our life here on earth as a race. He tells us to, "Run so as to win" (1 Cor 9:24). One way we can do this is to learn from those who have already won the prize, who have successfully finished the race. The saints, those who have gone before us, marked with the sign of faith, give us concrete examples of how to live in a relationship with the Holy Spirit. All of them experienced the presence and power of the Spirit. Their life histories are replete with stories of the Spirit's intervention through dreams, visions, locutions, inspirations, prophesy, healings, signs and wonders, and the like. In fact, as I mentioned in an earlier chapter, the heroic virtue and the unique vocations they lived, were more often than not, initially birthed through a concrete experience of the power of the Spirit. Their lives often mirrored the life of the early church, as recorded in the Acts of the Apostles. That is true even of those saints who by God's wisdom and perfect love lived for many years with little or no spiritual consolations.

In addition to the saints who have already gone home to the Lord, we will taste more of the life of the Spirit if we run with the saints that are still on earth. To learn to move more fully and deeply in the life of the Spirit, it is important to share one's life with others who desire to live the same way. If we are docile to the Spirit he will lead us to deeper fellowship with others who are serious about following Jesus. One of the central things the Spirit is doing in our day is bringing his people into a deeper experience of communion, in concrete expressions of various forms of community life.

7. Put on Love

One of my favorite passages is 1 Corinthians 13:1-13. That's the passage where St. Paul puts the whole of our spiritual journey in right order. He makes it clear that if I have every spiritual gift possible, and every kind of spiritual experience imaginable, "but have not love, I am nothing." He couldn't have put it more starkly. The experience of the Spirit, of his gifts and power, are for love. The Spirit is given to us so that we might fulfill the great commandment:

"Jesus answered, 'The first is, "Hear, O Israel: The Lord our God, the Lord is one; and you shall love the Lord your God with all your heart, and with all your soul, and with all your mind, and with all your strength." The second is this, "You shall love your neighbor as yourself." There is no other commandment greater than these'" (Mk 12:29-31).

The Spirit comes to conform us to the very life of God, to make us like him, so that we can live forever in the love of the Father, Son, and Holy Spirit: "So we know and believe the love God has for us. God is

love, and he who abides in love abides in God, and God abides in him"
(1 Jn 4:16).

Paul's perspective on love applies to every part of our lives, not just
to the possession and exercise of spiritual gifts. If I am the smartest wiz
kid on Wall Street, or if I am the most glamorous actress in
Hollywood, or if I am the wealthiest person in history, or if I've
achieved every single goal I have set for myself, but I have not love, I
AM NOTHING! In the end, when all is said and done, and history
has run its course, everything will pass away, and only love will remain:
"Love never ends" (1 Cor 13:8). If on that day, I am not found in him
and in his love, I too will pass away. This is what the Spirit most wants
us to know. He has come to draw us up into the love of God poured
out for us in Jesus of Nazareth so that we can live forever. That is the
difference the Spirit makes.

Notes

Introduction

1. George Weigel, *The Courage to Be Catholic* (Basic Books, New York, 2002), 32.

Chapter Two
A Whole New World

1. C.S. Lewis, *The Weight of Glory* (New York: MacMillan, 1949), 4.
2. John Paul II, "The Church wishes to spread Christ's fire in human hearts," *L'Osservatore Romano*, English Edition, 3 June 1998.
3. John Paul II, "Help laity be 'confessors of the faith.'" *L'Osservatore Romano*, English Edition, 10 March 1999, 5.
4. John Paul II, "The Church is missionary by her nature," *L'Osservatore Romano*, English Edition, 19 April 1995.

Chapter Three
The Challenge of Religious Experience

1. Mary Healy, "'Charismystics': Baptism in the Spirit and the Renewal of Catholic Spirituality," from Theological Symposium on the Catholic Charismatic Renewal After 35 Years, Franciscan University of Steubenville, 9/11/02.
2. Luke Timothy Johnson, *Religious Experience in Earliest Christianity* (Minneapolis: Fortress Press, 1998), 4-5.
3. *Tract on Psalm 118* 12:4; SC 347:76.
4. *The Confessions of St. Augustine* (London: Collier MacMillan Publishers, 1961), 130-31.
5. Healy.

6. John Paul II, *Incarnationis Mysterium*, no. 2.
7. John Paul II, *Christifideles Laici*, no. 2.
8. St. Bernard of Clairvaux, *Sermons on the Song of Songs* 1,11.
9. Pope John Paul II, "This is the day the Lord has made!" *L'Osservatore Romano*, English Edition, 3 June 1998.
10. "Mother Teresa's Mystical Experiences: Origin of Her Work," *Zenit News Service*, Rome, 29 November 2002.
11. "Mother Teresa's Mystical Experiences: Origin of Her Work."
12. Johnson, 60.
13. *Christifideles Laici*, no. 13.
14. Gary Zukav, *The Seat of The Soul* (New York: Simon & Schuster, 1989), 13.
15. Healy.
16. Hans Urs Von Balthasar, *Prayer* (San Francisco: Ignatius, 1986), 22.

Chapter Four
The Baptism in the Holy Spirit

1. Pope John Paul II, *"Then Peter stood up ..."*, (Vatican City: ICCRS, 2000), 51, 55.
2. *"Then Peter stood up ..."*, 123.
3. Francis Martin, "Baptism in the Spirit Thirty-five Years Later", Franciscan University of Steubenville, September 11-12, 2002.
4. *"Then Peter stood up ..."*, 76.
5. *CCC*, 1213.
6. Leo Josef Suenens, *The Holy Spirit, Life-Breath of the Church* (Belgium: FIAT, 2001), 90-92.
7. Kilian McDonnell and George Montague, *Fanning the Flame*, (Collegeville, Minn.: The Liturgical Press, 1991), 14-15.
8. Pope John XXIII, *Open the Windows*, (South Bend, Ind.: Greenlawn, 1989), 1.

9. *Open the Windows*, 8.
10. Pope Paul VI, from General Audience, 29 November 1972.
11. Pope John Paul II, from Angelus Address, 29 June 1995.
12. Pope John Paul II, from address to Bishops of Latin America, 21 October 1992.
13. Pope John Paul II, *L'Osservatore Romano*, English Edition, 3 June 1998, 2.

Chapter Five
Knowing Jesus as Lord

1. Joseph Ratzinger.
2. Pope John Paul II, *Letter to the Elderly*, November 1999.
3. *CCC*, no. 655.

Chapter Six
Freedom

1. Joseph Ratzinger, *"Above All, We Should Be Missionaries"* (Vatican City: Zenit News Service, September 30, 2001).
2. Lewis, 7.

Chapter Seven
A New Pentecost

1. Pope John Paul II, *L'Osservatore Romano* English Edition, 28 September 1994, 11.
2. Pope John Paul II, *L'Osservatore Romano* English Edition, 3 June 1998, 2.
3. Pope Paul VI, *Evangelii Nuntiandi*, 14.
4. Pope John Paul II, *Redemptoris Missio*, 5.
5. *Redemptoris Missio*, 21.

6. Joseph Ratzinger, *Inside the Vatican*, 3 June 1998.
7. Ibid.
8. Jospeh Ratzinger, L'Osservatore Romano, English Edition, 3 June 1998, p.16
9. Pope John Paul II, *L'Osservatore Romano*, English Edition, 3 June 1998.
10. Pope John Paul II, "The meaning of 'Spirit' in the Old Testament," General Audience, 3 January 1990.
11. Vatican Council II, *Lumen Gentium*, 12.
12. Cf., 1 Cor 12; Eph 4; 1 Cor 14; Rom 12.
13. *Evangelii Nuntiandi*, 70.
14. Pope John Paul II, *L'Osservatore Romano*, English Edition, 3 June 1998.
15. *St. Francis of Assisi, Writings and Early Biographies: English Omnibus of Sources for the Life of St. Francis*, (Chicago, Ill.: Fransciscan Herald Press, 1973), 810, 840.
16. Pope John Paul II, *L'Osservatore Romano*, English Edition, 28 September 1994, 11.
17. *Redemptoris Missio*, 92.
18. Final Message of Consistory of Cardinals of the Catholic Church, (Zenit.org), 24 May 2001.

Chapter Eight
An Eternal Perspective

1. *CCC,* 672.
2. Nicene Creed.
3. *CCC,* 678.
4. Lewis, 15.